ACTIVE LISTENING

113 TECHNIQUES & TIPS
TO IMPROVE YOUR RELATIONSHIPS THROUGH THE ART OF EMPATHIC COMMUNICATION

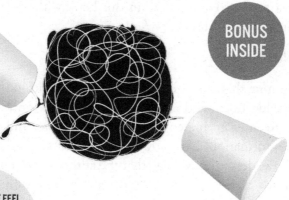

BONUS INSIDE

MAKE PEOPLE FEEL HEARD, UNDERSTOOD, AND VALUED BY ASKING THE RIGHT QUESTIONS

EMMA LEIGH WEBER

© **Copyright 2024 - All rights reserved.**

The content contained within this book may not be reproduced, duplicated, or transmitted without direct written permission from the author or the publisher.

Under no circumstances will any blame or legal responsibility be held against the publisher, or author, for any damages, reparation, or monetary loss due to the information contained within this book. Either direct or indirect. You are responsible for your own choices, actions, and results.

Legal Notice:

This book is copyright protected. This book is only for personal use. You cannot amend, distribute, sell, use, quote, or paraphrase any part of the content within this book without the consent of the author or publisher.

Disclaimer Notice:

Please note that the information contained within this document is for educational and entertainment purposes only. All effort has been executed to present accurate, up-to-date, and reliable complete information. No warranties of any kind are declared or implied. Readers acknowledge that the author is not engaging in the rendering of legal, financial, medical, or professional advice. The content within this book has been derived from various sources. Please consult a licensed professional before attempting any techniques outlined in this book.

By reading this document, the reader agrees that under to circumstances as the author is responsible for any losses, direct or indirect. Which are incurred as a result of the use of the information contained within this document, including, but not limited to, – errors, omissions, or inaccuracies.

Table of Contents

Introduction 5

Book 1: Listen with Your Heart 9
   The Art of Empathic Listening for Deeper
   Connections and Understanding

Book 2: The Power of Inquiry 51
   Mastering the Art of Asking the Right Questions
   for Improved Communication and Relationships

Book 3: Feedback Mastery 87
   The Art of Giving and Receiving Constructive
   Feedback for Personal and Professional Growth

Conclusion 129

Techniques & Tips Recap 135

Exclusive Bonuses 141

Resources 145

Introduction

Communication has become more convenient and efficient in today's fast-paced, technology-driven world. We have access to various tools and platforms that enable us to connect with others instantly, regardless of geographical distance. However, with this convenience comes the undeniable fact that the quality of our communication has suffered. In a world where texts, emails, and social media updates often replace face-to-face conversations, the art of truly listening and understanding one another has become a rarity.

At the heart of effective communication lies a skill that, when mastered, has the power to transform relationships, enhance collaboration, and foster personal growth – active listening. This essential skill requires more than just hearing the words spoken by others. Instead, it involves fully engaging in the conversation, empathizing with the speaker, and responding to demonstrate genuine understanding and interest. It is a skill that, when practiced and cultivated, can lead to deeper connections, better communication, and transformative self-improvement.

Active listening is a concept developed by theorists such as Carl Rogers and Richard Farson, who emphasized the importance of listening with empathy and understanding to facilitate effective communication and personal growth. Research has consistently shown that effective listening skills are critical for success in various aspects of life, including in one's relationships, professional endeavors, and personal development. Through introspection and self-discovery, it can help you acquire greater self-awareness and personal growth. In personal relationships, it fosters trust, empathy, and mutual understanding. In the workplace, it promotes collaboration, effective problem-solving, and a positive work environment.

At first glance, this concept may seem simple. However, it is a complex and multifaceted skill requiring deliberate practice and refinement. It goes beyond merely paying attention to the words spoken as it also involves comprehending the speaker's emotions, intentions, and subtext. It demands the listener to be fully present, suspending their judgments and preconceptions and focusing solely on understanding the speaker's perspective. In essence, active listening is a form of communication that goes beyond the surface level of exchanging words and delves into building genuine connections and understanding.

If you've ever found yourself struggling to connect with someone, whether it's a loved one, friend, or colleague, this book is for you. As someone who has faced the challenges of being an introvert with ADHD, I know firsthand how difficult it can be to form meaningful relationships. My fascination with the intricate workings of human relationships led me to pursue degrees in psychology and sociology. As a counselor, speaker, and author, I want to share what I learned with you.

Through my personal experiences, I've understood the importance of effective communication and how it can make or break a relationship. I've written this book to share the insights and techniques that have helped me and can help you improve your communication skills and relationships. Every day we converse with others, and every missed opportunity to genuinely connect due to poor communication skills is a lost chance to deepen our relationships and understanding. Don't let another day go by without taking the first step towards better communication and stronger connections.

In this book, I'll guide you through the art of active listening. You will find 65 techniques, tips, and strategies on how to listen with your heart and make people feel heard, understood, and valued peppered throughout the entire book. It's intentionally designed this way to serve as your guide along each step of the process.

This book is structured into three sub-books, each focusing on a different aspect of active listening to provide a comprehensive understanding of this essential skill. Each will delve into the theory, techniques, and practical applications of its respective topic, enabling you to develop a well-rounded and in-depth understanding of active listening, as a whole.

In the first sub-book, we dive into the powerful practice of empathic listening, which is a foundation of active listening and the key to establishing deeper connections and fostering a greater understanding of others. Unlike other types of listening, empathic listening goes beyond just hearing the words spoken; it requires cultivating self-awareness and emotional intelligence. I'll teach you how to create a safe space for open communication, provide various techniques, as well as present real-life applications of empathic listening in personal relationships, the workplace, and challenging situations.

The second sub-book emphasizes the crucial role of asking questions in effective communication, especially after engaging in empathic listening. By posing thoughtful and meaningful questions, you can better understand the person you're speaking with and forge stronger bonds. I'll share with you various questioning types. I will also introduce five golden rules to guide you in crafting the most impactful questions. These guidelines will ensure your inquiries engage the other person and contribute to a more meaningful and insightful dialogue.

The third and final sub-book discusses the significant role of providing feedback in active listening. This section will cover various types, purposes, and contexts of feedback, emphasizing the importance of cultivating a culture of trust and openness that encourages it. I will introduce the SBI (Situation, Behavior, Impact) model as a valuable tool for giving constructive feedback. I'll provide strategies for overcoming common challenges encountered when giving feedback, ensuring it is helpful and well-received. On the other end of the spectrum, I'll also discuss the value of receiving feedback and tackling the issues that arise when asking for it. To support you in making the most of the feedback you receive, I will guide you through the process of transforming it into action. This includes creating a feedback action plan and regularly monitoring your progress to ensure you stay on track and achieve your goals.

As you read and engage with the content of this book, you will discover the transformative power of active listening. Throughout each page, you will find practical exercises designed to help you apply the concepts and techniques discussed in your daily life. These exercises will reinforce your understanding of active listening and provide opportunities to practice and refine your skills in real-life situations. This comprehensive guide Is an invaluable resource in your journey toward mastering this skill and unlocking its countless benefits in all aspects of your life.

Whether you're looking to deepen your relationships, improve your communication at work, or become a better listener, this book has something for you. By practicing the art of active listening, you'll see significant improvements in your relationships and overall communication skills. So, let's dive in and start your journey toward mastering this skill.

Book 1

Listen with Your Heart

The Art of Empathic Listening for Deeper Connections and Understanding

Table of Contents

Chapter 1: The Power of Empathic Listening.......................13
    Benefits of Empathic Listening..14
    Empathic vs. Other Types of Listening...............................18
    Barriers to Empathic Listening..21

Chapter 2: Developing the Foundations 23
    Empathy 23
    Trust 28
    Confidentiality 28
    Non-Judgment 28
    Safe Environment..29
    Reflective Exercises 32

Chapter 3: Putting it into Practice..35
    Essential Tips to Listen Empathically 35
    Empathic Listening in Action..41

Chapter 1:
The Power of Empathic Listening

Empathic listening allows you to genuinely connect with others by hearing their words and grasping their emotions. Through wholeheartedly engaging and striving to understand the viewpoint of the people you are speaking with, you can elevate your relationships and enhance communication in your personal and professional lives. In this chapter, I will break down the nitty-gritty of empathic listening; discussing its significance, and differentiating it from other listening styles. Additionally, I will share common obstacles that can impede your empathic listening abilities and practical solutions for overcoming them.

The capacity to empathize is an often overlooked yet innate talent that nearly all humans possess. Some people may argue that some do not seem empathetic, such as famous serial killers like Ted Bundy. However, only a small percentage of the population lacks empathy. It is contrary to what philosophers have argued in the past. For centuries, prominent thinkers, including the renowned Thomas Hobbes, have propagated the notion that humans are fundamentally self-centered and driven by individualism and selfishness. Nevertheless, compelling scientific evidence has come to light recently, unveiling our innate capacity for empathy as well.

20th-century research in neuroscience indicates that when we empathize, the neural structures activated are the same as those involved in directly experiencing the emotion (Singer & Lamm, 2009). It suggests a physiological connection between empathy and our ability to share the feelings of others. On the other hand, evolutionary biologists have demonstrated that, like our primate relatives, humans are social animals who have naturally evolved to be empathic and cooperative. Based on these studies alone, it is clear that our empathic tendencies are just as powerful as our selfish impulses and that most of humanity is born with the ability to empathize and connect with others.

However, despite our innate capacity to empathize, we are currently confronting an empathy deficit, particularly in the workplace. It refers to a lack of understanding and compassion towards others, both at the individual and societal levels. According to a Forbes article, the empathy deficit in the workplace can significantly impact an organization's bottom line (Bruce, 2022). Empathy is a significant component of social life, evident in numerous daily interactions. A world devoid of it would be cold and indifferent. This growing problem underscores the importance of developing empathic listening skills to create a more compassionate and understanding world, personally and professionally.

Benefits of Empathic Listening

Empathic listening is a form of active, responsive listening that involves the listener to be fully present, attentive, and open to the speaker's perspective. This type of listening goes beyond merely hearing the words spoken and seeks to understand the underlying emotions, intentions, and context behind the message. Empathic listeners utilize verbal and non-verbal cues, ask thought-provoking questions, and maintain eye contact to demonstrate understanding and support. It holds great importance due to its numerous implications on one's personal and professional relationships, communication abilities, and overall health and wellness. It can positively impact our lives in several ways, and its benefits can be neatly organized into two interconnected categories: personal and relational.

Personal

At first glance, it's easy to assume that the benefits of empathic listening are primarily relational, given that it involves the interaction between a listener and a speaker. However, there's more to this powerful tool than meets the eye. As you learn more about empathic listening, you'll uncover an unexpected aspect of its impact—personal development. Contrary to common belief, empathic listening doesn't just enhance one's relationships; it also has the potential to ignite an internal journey of self-discovery, emotional growth, and inner harmony. Intrigued? Read on as I enumerate the various facets of this transformative process and unveil the surprising personal benefits that await you.

Enhances Emotional Intelligence

Empathic listening helps you develop your ability to recognize, understand, and manage your emotions and those of others. It sharpens your intuition and gut instincts. This emotional intelligence is crucial for navigating complex social situations and maintaining healthy relationships, such as in challenging work environments or when dealing with diverse groups of colleagues. When you listen empathetically to someone's concerns, you can better comprehend their emotions and needs. You become more adept at recognizing subtle cues and non-verbal communication. This enables you to understand people's intentions and motivations better as you provide appropriate support and encouragement.

Fosters Personal Growth and Development

Constant exposure to diverse ideas and experiences stimulates personal growth and intellectual development. Picture yourself attending a community event and encountering people from various cultural backgrounds and belief systems. Through this, you immerse yourself in their stories and experiences, expanding your worldview and nurturing empathy for others.

Empathic listening allows you to gain insights into different perspectives and experiences, fostering a more compassionate outlook on life. It allows you to widen your knowledge and understanding of the world by encouraging you to be more aware of social issues and take on a more active role. This openness to new information and experiences enables you to adapt more effectively to changing circumstances.

Strengthens Self-Esteem

By practicing empathic listening, you actively engage with the speaker and demonstrate a genuine interest in their thoughts and feelings. This focused attention and emotional investment in the conversation can lead to a sense of happiness, knowing that you have positively impacted someone's life by truly understanding their emotions and experiences. Being on the receiving end of empathic listening can also be an empowering and validating experience if you're the speaker, as it feels good to know that you are heard, understood, and respected. Empathic listening acknowledges the value of thoughts and emotions, reinforcing the idea that experiences and perspectives matter. Your self-esteem and confidence may improve as you recognize your ability to connect with others and provide meaningful support while empowering the speaker to express themselves more openly and authentically.

Relational

Imagine a world where your interactions are infused with genuine understanding, deep connections, and mutual support—a world where the bonds you forge are resilient and authentic. This vision is within your grasp when you embrace and practice empathic listening. I will now show you the transformative power of empathic listening, highlighting its role in strengthening connections and improving relationships.

Builds Trust and Rapport

Trust is the foundation of any strong personal or professional relationship. When you practice empathic listening, you create a safe and supportive environment that encourages people to share their thoughts, feelings, and experiences comfortably. This openness promotes honesty and vulnerability, which eventually leads to emotional intimacy. The mutual exchange of understanding fosters a stronger emotional bond and a more fulfilling connection between individuals. For example, when a close friend struggles with a personal issue, empathizing with them will help them express their feelings openly without fear of judgment or dismissal. You can attentively validate their emotions, which makes them feel heard and understood, and in turn, deepens your bond.

Improves Communication

Conflict is a natural and inevitable part of any relationship, and how you handle these conflicts can significantly impact the health and longevity of your connections. Listening to each other's perspectives and putting yourselves in each other's shoes can help parties involved in a disagreement find common ground and work toward a mutually beneficial solution. Consider a situation where two family members are embroiled in a heated argument over a sensitive issue. Both parties can step back from their entrenched positions and genuinely try to understand each other's perspectives. They can do this by taking a breather and listening to what the other has to say. This paves the way for finding common ground and resolving the conflict amicably.

Boost Mental Health

Empathic listening also promotes feelings of social support, reduces feelings of isolation, and provides a space for emotional expression and processing. Picture a support group for individuals coping with a shared challenge, such as grief or addiction. As group members practice empathic listening, they create a safe environment for emotional expression and processing. This support network strengthens interpersonal connections and improves emotional well-being by facilitating the processing and releasing of negative emotions.

Now that you've explored the incredible benefits of empathic listening, it's time to learn how to differentiate it from other types of listening. While all forms of listening involve receiving and processing information, empathic listening stands out as it delves deeper into understanding the emotions, intentions, and context behind the message. You'll see more of this in the next section.

Empathic vs. Other Types of Listening

Aside from empathic, there are other types of listening. They are appreciative, informational, and passive listening. Each one has a unique purpose and approach and knowing what they are will help you know which one is appropriate to use in your conversations. In this section, I will expand on the key distinctions that set an empathic listener apart and provide examples of how it differs from other forms of listening.

Informational Listening

Informational listening is a focused and purposeful type of listening that aims to gather and comprehend specific information or details. It involves actively listening to extract facts, instructions, or data with clarity and accuracy. Informational listening requires a high level of concentration, attentiveness, and the ability to discern relevant information from a speaker's message. As opposed to emphatic listening, this type is more analytical in nature as it demands the listener to process, retain, and utilize the information that they were presented. It is often utilized in educational settings, professional environments, or when seeking guidance or directions such as a student digesting a lecture, an employee absorbing a presentation, or a citizen following a news broadcast.

Appreciative Listening

Appreciative listening is a form of active listening that focuses on seeking out and appreciating the positive aspects of what is being communicated and shared. A great example of this is when you watch a show such as the opera, a movie, or even theater. Visualize it for a moment.

Imagine you're at a symphony, lost in the sea of harmonious sound cascading from the stage. You're not focused on the individual notes or listening hard to analyze the composition. Instead, you're letting the music wash over you. It's as if every molecule around you dances to the melody, and for a moment, you lose yourself in the beauty of it all. You're enjoying the rhythm that pulls at your heartstrings.

As opposed to empathic listening, appreciative listening is all about enjoyment and aesthetic pleasure. With this type of listening, you're a spectator and not an active participant.

Passive Listening

Passive listening is like standing in a bustling city square, watching life's countless dramas unfold. It refers to the act of hearing without actively engaging or processing the information being conveyed. The conversations are buzzing around you, but you're an outsider, uninvolved and disconnected. You hear the sounds and words, but they leave no lasting impression.

It is a more passive and superficial form of listening, where the listener may be physically present but mentally disengaged. We often implore this in moments of fatigue or disinterest. It might be during a dull meeting, when your mind wanders off to your evening plans, or in the middle of a lecture that doesn't spark your curiosity, and you find yourself daydreaming. We merely hear; we do not truly listen. Unlike empathic listening, with this type, the primary focus is on hearing the words being spoken, but little effort is made to comprehend, retain, or respond to the message.

Evaluative Listening

Evaluative listening is a form of listening that involves critically analyzing and assessing the message being communicated. It focuses on evaluating the accuracy, credibility, and quality of the information presented. During evaluative listening, the listener applies their own judgment, knowledge, and expertise to form opinions or make assessments about the speaker's ideas, arguments, or claims. This type of listening often occurs in academic or professional settings, where the listener seeks to determine the validity, reliability, and soundness of the information. Unlike empathic listening which requires on to take into account the speakers emotions, evaluative listening requires a discerning and analytical mindset, as well as the ability to separate personal biases from objective evaluation.

Selective Listening

Also known as biased listening, selective listening refers to the act of focusing only on specific parts or aspects of a message while ignoring or disregarding other parts. It involves consciously or unconsciously filtering out information that is deemed less relevant or interesting to the listener. Selective listening can occur due to distractions, personal biases, preoccupations, or a lack of attention. Unlike empathic listening which prioritizes understanding the speaker's emotions and experiences and validating their perspective, selective listening involves filtering out certain parts of the message based on personal interest or relevance without thought or regard about creating an emotional connection with the speaker.

Barriers to Empathic Listening

The remarkable benefits of empathic listening should undoubtedly inspire you to start practicing it in your daily interactions. However, it is not without challenges. There are several barriers that may hinder your ability to listen empathically and tap into its full potential. Before you can utilize the skill successfully, you must be aware of these obstacles and prepare yourself to overcome them.

Let's take a comprehensive exploration of these common hindrances. Fear not, as we'll also offer insightful tips and guidance that will be useful in overcoming these barriers in the chapters to come. This way, you'll be well-equipped to effectively practice and in turn, improve your skills.

- *Prejudice and Bias:* These can manifest as stereotypes, preconceived notions, or assumptions about others based on factors such as race, gender, age, or socioeconomic status. These biases can prevent you from truly understanding and empathizing with the speaker's perspective as they can cloud your judgments.
- *Emotional reactivity:* It refers to the tendency to become overwhelmed when confronted with strong emotions, either your own or the speaker's. When you are emotionally reactive, you may experience intense emotions that take a long time to subside. This can make it difficult to think clearly or make rational decisions, especially in stressful situations. It can even lead to impulsivity as you act in the heat of the moment which you might regret later.
- *Distractions:* Disturbances can be external, such as noise or interruptions, or internal, like wandering thoughts or preoccupations. These distractions hinder your ability to

listen well and emphatically since you are not fully engaged with the speaker. As I said earlier, empathic listening entails active engagement.

- **Impatience:** Impatience can cause you to interrupt the speaker, rush to judgment, or prematurely offer solutions without fully understanding the speaker's perspective. Imagine you are the speaker; you certainly would feel hurt or disrespected when somebody suddenly interrupts you midway. It goes to show that your feelings or opinions are less important. This applies to anybody, so you should be more patient when practicing empathic listening.
- **Defensiveness:** This occurs when you perceive the speaker's message as a personal attack or criticism. It can lead to emotional reactivity and an inability to listen empathically as you focus on defending your position or feelings.

Chapter 2:
Developing the Foundations

A handful of essential elements come together to form the very foundation of empathic listening. These key components include empathy, emotional intelligence, trust, and a safe environment. These intricacies define empathic listening and play a vital role in understanding your unique approach to it. Establishing these foundations is a valuable step towards mastering and using this skill effectively in your life. Let's discuss them one by one.

Empathy

Empathy is often confused with sympathy, but it is not exactly the same. While empathy involves understanding and sharing the emotions of others, sympathy is simply feeling sorry for someone. The latter may provide a sense of comfort, but it does not foster the same level of connection and understanding that empathy does.

To help clarify the distinction between the two, let us ponder on the situation Brené Brown, a research professor and author, provided as an illustration. During a conference in 2013, she asked the audience to imagine a person who has fallen into a dark hole and feels overwhelmed. Brown suggested that a sympathetic response in this situation would be to say, "Whoa! That is bad. I am sorry you are down there. Do you want a sandwich?" On the other hand, an empathetic response would be, "I know what it is like down here. It is tough. And you are not alone."

Here we can see that empathy is "I am feeling *with* you," while sympathy is "I feel *for* you," which are two entirely different things. Brown's example of the person in the dark hole highlights this distinction, with the sympathetic response merely acknowledging the situation and offering a simple solution. In contrast, the empathic response involves actively connecting with the person and acknowledging their struggles.

Before you can fully apply empathic listening, you first need to be able to feel with others and exercise empathy. Based on the example above, you can empathize with another person by acknowledging their feelings. Let them know that you hear and understand their emotions. Though it can be as simple as saying, "I understand why you would feel that way," trust me, it is powerful in deepening connections. Be patient. Empathy takes time and effort. Don't rush into things or solve the problem quickly. Instead, take your time with the conversation to really understand the person's thoughts and feelings. Through this, you get to empathize better as you get to see the reasons for their behaviors, opinions, or emotions.

Maintaining an Empathic Mindset

Empathic mindset is the result of consistently practicing empathy. With this mindset, empathizing with others become second nature. It no longer feels like an obligation but rather an act that you do genuinely and willingly.

To develop and maintain an empathic mindset, you need to foster self-awareness. This allows you to regulate your emotions and reactions, ensuring you remain open and receptive to the speaker's feelings and experiences. In cultivating self-awareness and self-regulation, consider practicing mindfulness meditation or journaling. Both activities can help you better understand your emotions, thoughts, and reactions, enabling you to identify and address any barriers to empathy.

When you are self-aware, you can recognize personal biases. You have to avoid letting these get ahead of you and affect your ability to empathize with others negatively. One way to do this is to confront them honestly about your prejudices. Working to challenge them can also help you understand why you have these in the first place.

Keep in mind that it's not only you, but every individual, who carries a set of biases and assumptions. This is why an empathic mindset requires being open and non-judgmental toward others. This means suspending judgment and allowing the speaker to express their feelings and experiences without fear of criticism or dismissal. Try to put yourself in the shoes of someone with a different belief or opinion and imagine their experiences, emotions, and reasoning. Ask yourself, "How would I feel in this situation?" This can help you understand their perspective and emotions better.

Practicing empathy in everyday situations is essential to create and maintain an empathic mindset. It means actively seeking opportunities to empathize with others, whether a colleague, a friend, or a stranger. Although humans are born capable of empathizing, it's also considered a skill. This means that it can be developed and refined over time. The more you practice, you will see the greater impact of empathy on your life. When you continue to develop your empathic mindset, you will become a better listener and a more compassionate and supportive friend, family member, and colleague.

Emotional Intelligence

Managing your own emotions is crucial when practicing and cultivating an empathic mindset. However, recognizing and responding to the emotions of others is as important. This is where enhancing emotional intelligence comes into play. Emotional intelligence (EI) is the ability to recognize, understand, and manage our own emotions as well as the emotions of others. The way you respond to a person is greatly affected by your emotional intelligence. Improving this can help you confidently engage and connect with others as you gain a clearer understanding of their emotions.

By improving emotional intelligence, you will be better equipped to ensure you concentrate on verbal and non-verbal cues (such as tone of voice, facial expressions, and body language), respond with compassion, support, and appropriate action, as well as make better decisions.

Enhancing your emotional intelligence requires you to focus on several key aspects. They are:

- *Emotional awareness:* Develop the ability to identify and comprehend your own emotions, strengths, weaknesses, and triggers. This understanding will allow you to be more in tune with your emotional state and better equipped to respond to different situations.
- *Emotional management:* Learn to handle your emotions, responses, and impulses effectively to remain composed and adaptable in varying circumstances. This skill helps you maintain emotional stability and react appropriately to challenges or stressors.
- *Motivation:* Stay driven and committed to your goals, even in the face of challenges or setbacks. Cultivating intrinsic motivation helps you persevere and maintain focus on your objectives, contributing to overall success.
- *Social skills:* Develop effective communication, conflict resolution, and collaboration skills to build and maintain strong relationships with others. Mastering these skills enables you to work efficiently in teams, navigate social situations easily, and foster a positive environment.
- *Emotional expression:* Learn to communicate your emotions openly and honestly while also being mindful of others' feelings. Effective emotional expression fosters trust and understanding in your relationships, encouraging open dialogue and support.

It is important to understand that emotional intelligence is an ongoing process of self-awareness and self-improvement. With that in mind, I have compiled a list of ten thought-provoking questions designed to help you assess your current level of emotional intelligence. Reflecting on your responses to these questions will offer valuable insights into your emotional awareness, empathy, and ability to connect with others. Remember, emotional intelligence can be developed over time, so use these questions as a starting point for self-reflection and personal growth.

1. Am I aware of my emotions and able to identify them accurately?
2. Can I recognize and understand the emotions of others, even when they are not explicitly stated?
3. Do I know how to manage my own emotions, especially in stressful or challenging situations?
4. Am I able to maintain a positive attitude and motivate myself to achieve my goals, even when facing obstacles?
5. Can I effectively manage conflict and navigate difficult conversations with others?
6. Do I know how to adapt my communication style based on the emotional state and needs of the person I am interacting with?
7. Am I able to build and maintain strong, trusting relationships with others?
8. Do I practice empathic listening and genuinely try to understand others' perspectives, even if they differ from mine?
9. Can I work collaboratively and effectively within a team, understanding and managing the emotions and dynamics of the group?
10. Am I able to take constructive criticism and feedback without becoming defensive or taking it personally?

Trust

Trust serves as the bedrock for meaningful interactions. Both parties can engage in more authentic, transparent, and insightful exchanges when it is established in conversations. Central to the development of trust are two fundamental elements - confidentiality and non-judgment. These are the mechanisms through which a safe environment is fostered, encouraging individuals to share personal thoughts, feelings, and experiences without fear of exposure or criticism.

Confidentiality

When you feel secure knowing that your personal thoughts, feelings, and experiences will remain confidential, you are more likely to open up and share your innermost emotions. Opening up and showing your vulnerability to someone you trust is easier because you don't have to worry about criticism or exposure. This resonates deeply because, as social beings, humans innately crave validation and are often concerned about their image and how others perceive them.

Non-Judgment

Knowing that you are accepted and not judged allows you to lower your defenses and express yourself more fully, thereby strengthening your interpersonal connections. Aside from this, when you feel safe and supported, you are more likely to reciprocate the empathy and trust that you have been given. The parties involved can take turns sharing, reinforcing the empathic bond. This promotes a cycle of empathy and compassion, eventually creating a safe environment.

This can be observed in the therapeutic settings, where therapists maintain strict therapist-client confidentiality to ensure a trusting environment. This confidentiality encourages clients to share their emotions and experiences openly, leading to a deeper understanding and connection between the therapist and the client. In a workplace setting, managers can create an atmosphere of trust by prioritizing confidentiality and non-judgment when addressing employee concerns. It's as simple as reprimanding and criticizing in private. This allows employees to communicate their feelings and needs without fear of retribution or ridicule.

Safe Environment

Cultivating trust is a precursor to fostering a safe environment. Trust among individuals creates an atmosphere where they feel safe to express their emotions and ideas without fear of judgment or criticism. These two concepts, although separate, are intrinsically connected.

To further convince and motivate you to prioritize trust and empathy, it is essential to understand the impact of cultivating a secure and supportive environment. The following benefits showcase how investing in trust can transform both personal and professional relationships, emphasizing the importance of creating a safe environment and promoting a culture of honesty and transparency:

- *Psychological safety:* People feel secure in expressing their thoughts and emotions without fear of judgment or negative consequences.
- *Emotional support:* In a supportive environment, the listener genuinely cares for the speaker's well-being.
- *Mutual respect:* An environment of trust is characterized by mutual respect, where both parties acknowledge each other's perspectives and feelings.
- *Accountability and responsibility:* Individuals take ownership of their actions and decisions, fostering a sense of reliability and dependability in a safe environment.
- *Enhanced problem-solving:* Trust and empathy in a safe environment can lead to more productive problem-sol-

ving, as individuals feel more comfortable sharing ideas and working together to find solutions.

Strategies for Fostering a Safe Environment

Now that you understand the importance and benefits of fostering a safe atmosphere that encourages empathic listening, it's time to explore how to build trust and create a safe listening environment. Implementing the following strategies can help you establish an environment where the speaker feels psychologically safe and comfortable in sharing their thoughts and emotions.

Offer affirmative responses and feedback that demonstrate your engagement. This can be done through non-verbal cues, such as nodding or verbal affirmations like "I see" or "I understand." Don't let the conversation die down or lead to an awkward silence. Instead of merely saying supporting statements, you can also throw in some questions that invite deeper exploration of their experiences and feelings. You'll find the second sub-book helpful since I have included techniques for better framing your questions.

Express empathy as you listen. Remember, the person you speak with shows you their vulnerable side. Instead of using this moment of weakness to criticize the person further, show them that you are "feeling" with them. Express that you genuinely care about them and utilize empathic statements to communicate your understanding of their situation and emotions. This should also serve as a reminder that you must be mindful of your own emotions and reactions during the conversation. Practice self-awareness and self-regulation to prevent your emotions from interfering with your ability to listen empathically.

Build rapport. Lastly, look at this opportunity to not only build an environment of trust but also to establish rapport. Remind yourself that you are not listening passively and, instead, seeking to connect with the speaker on a personal level. You can do this by finding common ground or sharing relatable experiences. This can help create a bond of trust and understanding, making the speaker feel more at ease in sharing their thoughts and feelings.

Be Dependable and consistent in your actions and words. Once they are done sharing, show that you can be trusted by following through on promises and maintaining confidentiality. Never share with others what you have learned about the person without their permission as a form of respect.

Following the tips I shared, I can assure you that this will not be the last conversation you'll have with them, as they will see that you are trustworthy enough for them to share their innermost thoughts and feelings with.

Activities to Further Cultivate Empathy

If you still find listening empathically challenging, you can refer to the exercises I have included below. These are intended to be completed individually or in pairs, providing opportunities to practice empathy in various contexts. I hope you will gain a deeper understanding of empathy and develop practical strategies for incorporating it into your everyday interactions by doing these exercises.

- *Reflection question:* Consider a recent situation where you may have displayed sympathy instead of empathy. How could you have responded with empathy instead? Write down your thoughts.
- *Roleplay exercise:* Partner with a friend or family member and take turns roleplaying as the person who has fallen into the dark hole from Brené Brown's example. Have the other person practice responding empathetically to the situation.
- *Journaling exercise:* At the end of each day, briefly describe a situation where you practiced empathy or could have practiced empathy. Describe the emotions and per-

spectives of the person you empathized with and how you felt during the interaction.
- ***Observation exercise:*** Spend a day observing your interactions with others and noting when you respond with sympathy or empathy. Try to notice patterns in your behavior and identify areas for improvement.
- ***Empathy challenge:*** Pick a news story or a social issue that you have strong opinions about. Research the perspectives of people who hold opposing views and try to empathize with their feelings and experiences. Write a short paragraph summarizing your understanding of their perspective and emotions.
- ***Visualization exercise:*** Close your eyes and imagine a person you know who is going through a difficult time. Visualize their emotions and experiences as vividly as possible. Practice putting yourself in their shoes and feeling the emotions they may be experiencing. When you are done, consider reaching out to this person to offer empathetic support.

Reflective Exercises

As you develop your empathy, emotional intelligence, and trust-building skills, take the time to reflect on your personal growth and progress as well. The following reflective exercises are designed to help you think about your experiences, emotions, and behaviors concerning these skills. Use these questions as a guide to gain insights and continue enhancing your abilities.

- Think about a recent conversation where you tried to practice empathy. How did you recognize and understand the emotions of the speaker?
- Recall a situation where you responded to someone with compassion, support, and appropriate action. What steps did you take to provide the most effective response?

- Consider your journey in cultivating emotional intelligence through self-awareness and self-regulation. What strategies have you used to develop your emotional intelligence?
- Reflect on a time when you recognized your personal biases, emotions, and assumptions during a conversation. How did this awareness impact your ability to empathize and build trust with others?
- How has incorporating mindfulness and self-reflection into your daily routine helped enhance your empathy and emotional intelligence?
- Describe a situation where you encouraged an open, non-judgmental perspective while interacting with others. What techniques did you use to create this environment?
- Think about a conversation where you maintained confidentiality and a non-judgmental attitude. Why was this important in building trust and promoting empathy and emotional intelligence?

Chapter 3:
Putting it into Practice

Now that we're done talking about the 'what', it's now time to talk about the 'how.' So roll up your sleeves and take a plunge into the practical application of empathic listening. Building on the foundational knowledge presented in the earlier chapters, we will now explore strategies, techniques, and real-life scenarios to help you become an effective empathic listener. This chapter is designed to provide a comprehensive understanding of applying empathy in your everyday interactions. Through examples, exercises, and reflective prompts, you will learn how to strengthen your empathic listening muscles so that you can attune to others' emotions, and cultivate compassion for those around you. By the end of this chapter, you will have the tools and confidence to approach discussions with an open heart and mind. You will be ready to engage in meaningful and supportive dialogues that empowers you and your conversation partners.

Essential Tips to Listen Empathically

This guide is tailored to provide actionable strategies and tips to help you better understand, connect, and communicate with others on a deeper level. Through this, you can equip yourself with the tools to truly hear and comprehend the emotions and experiences of others.

Give Your Full Attention

In today's fast-paced, hyper-connected world, countless distractions compete for your attention. From your mobile phone alerts to your email notifications, your attention is getting pulled into multiple directions. There are more noise that you need to filter than ever. But when you're talking to someone, you can't allow these distractions to take hold of your attention. Merely appearing attentive in a conversation will not help you connect with others on a deeper level. People can sense when you are not truly present.

Preoccupation can significantly hinder empathic listening, as it may cause you to focus on internal thoughts or distractions rather than the message being communicated. It can result in an incomplete or inaccurate understanding of the conversation and potentially inappropriate responses. Consider how it feels to talk to someone whose mind is clearly elsewhere—perhaps they keep checking their phone, glancing over your shoulder, or looking at the time. You can't help but think that you and what you have to say don't matter to them at that particular moment. Whatever distracts them is evidently more important than speaking with you, which is not a pleasant feeling. In turn, you start to lose interest in the conversation and might not engage with that person again anytime soon.

A famous anecdote illustrates this concept: A New York columnist, suspecting that a particular socialite was so absorbed with impressing her guests that she failed to truly listen to them, arrived late to her party and announced he had murdered his wife and struggled to hide the body. The hostess, seemingly oblivious, cheerfully welcomed him and declared that the party could now begin (Pfeiffer, 1998).

As technology is so advanced to the point that everyone has a smartphone, shutting them down together with other distractions becomes more important than ever. Research shows that even the mere presence of a smartphone can reduce the quality of a conversation—even if it's just sitting at the table.

In a 2014 study called "The iPhone Effect," researchers observed 200 participants in a coffee shop as they conversed for about ten minutes. They specifically noted whether a mobile device was used, touched, or placed on the table during the conversation. Afterward, participants were asked to respond to questions and statements designed to measure feelings of connection and empathic concern. The results revealed that if either participant used their phone or placed it on the table, the conversation was rated as less fulfilling than conversations without mobile devices present. The researchers concluded that digital devices represent people's broader social network, and their presence triggers a constant urge to seek information, check for communication, and direct thoughts somewhere else.

If someone wants to talk when you're preoccupied or unable to pause, let them know and suggest talking later. You can say, "I apologize. I'm currently occupied and wouldn't be able to focus on our conversation. Can we speak later? I'd like to ensure I can devote my complete attention to you." Once you are free to speak with them, demonstrate that they have your undivided attention. Remove all possible distractions, such as putting away your laptop or turning off the TV. These small actions significantly enhance your presence, help you avoid distractions, and show the other person that you care enough to focus solely on them.

Another way that you can show your attentiveness is through your body language. This can speak volumes about your attentiveness and empathy. Maintain eye contact, lean slightly towards the speaker, and use open body language, such as uncrossing your arms and legs. Nodding occasionally can also show that you are engaged in the conversation. These nonverbal cues help convey that you are genuinely interested in what the person is saying and are fully present.

Giving someone your undivided attention is a sign of respect. If you genuinely care about the person you are conversing with, offer them the priceless gift of your presence, not just physically but mentally, as well. In this way, you can communicate more effectively.

Avoid Interrupting

This tip is a challenge for me as someone with ADHD, where tendencies to interrupt are often a part of the condition. If you're the same, keep in mind that when you interrupt someone or finish their sentences, you inadvertently communicate that your thoughts are more important than theirs. It can leave them feeling snubbed and undervalued. That's why even if you think you know what they're about to say or have a great piece of advice, let them finish their thought. Interruptions can be perceived as an attempt to establish control and power in a conversation (Huls, 2000). In fact, successful interruptions often lead to the interrupter taking control of the conversation, potentially causing the speaker to feel disregarded or disrespected. Through this, you disrupt the natural flow of conversation and violate the basic organization of a social relationship established in a conversation-based interaction environment (Sacks, Schegloff, & Jefferson, 1974).

The negative effects of interrupting can have a profound impact on relationships and communication. When you consistently interrupt someone, you risk damaging the trust and rapport that is vital for building strong connections. For one, this can lead to miscommunication, as allowing the speaker to finish their thoughts is crucial for understanding the intended message. Moreover, constant interruptions can cause frustration and resentment, which may strain the relationship further. Practice patience and let the speaker share their feelings, ideas, and perspectives without interference.

Refrain from Offering Unsolicited Advice

When a person explicitly requests guidance from someone else, it's clear that they are seeking advice. However, in many situations, whether a speaker is asking for advice or not depends on how the listener interprets the conversation (Horowitz et al., 2000). It is important to remember that not every conversation about problems requires a solution. When people engage in discussions about their troubles and worries, their goal might be to gain sympathy and understanding or to connect with a supportive listener rather than explicitly seeking advice. In short, they just need a listening ear and an empathetic response.

Providing unsolicited advice can have negative effects on a relationship. On the part of the advice-giver, they might feel overburdened. The receiver, on the other hand, might feel disempowered or undermined.

Instead of jumping in with advice, practice active listening and provide emotional support. Make sure the speaker feels heard and understood before considering whether to offer any guidance. If you think you have valuable input, let them finish speaking first, then ask for permission before sharing your thoughts. By doing so, you respect the speaker's boundaries and focus on empathy.

Reflect, Summarize, and Encourage Elaboration

Taking the time to reflect and summarize what the speaker has shared not only confirms that you've genuinely grasped their message but also demonstrates your attentive and eager engagement in understanding them. For instance, after they've shared their thoughts, you may respond with, "If I'm getting this right, you felt hurt when your co-worker brushed off your idea during the meeting, right?" This approach feels more relatable and helps build a stronger connection with the speaker.

In tandem with reflecting and summarizing, it's essential to encourage the speaker to elaborate on their thoughts and feelings. Sometimes, people might hesitate to fully express themselves, fearing judgment or misunderstanding. Questions such as, "Can you tell me more about what happened?" or "How did that make you feel?" can help them feel more comfortable in sharing and opening up with you.

Allow for Silence

In conversations, silence is often overlooked and relegated to the realm of awkwardness and discomfort. Yet, it can be a powerful tool in empathic listening. It allows for moments of reflection and emotional processing to deepen the connection between conversational partners. In fact, many cultures view silence as a sign of respect and reverence, which signals acknowledgment for the speaker and their experience. This gesture of humility and deference can make the speaker feel heard, acknowledged, and appreciated.

When you allow silence to occupy the spaces between words, you create room for introspection and contemplation. As listeners, you demonstrate your willingness to let the speaker take the time they need to gather their thoughts and express themselves more fully. Emotions can be complex or overwhelming, and articulating them can be challenging. When you start embracing silence in your conversations, you allow the speaker to navigate their emotional landscape, unearth buried feelings, and find the words that best capture their experience.

However, it's worth noting that there's a difference between the easy silence that fosters trust and connection and the awkward silence that can sometimes arise in conversations. The key lies in understanding the context, reading the speaker's body language, and being attuned to their emotional state. You can signal your active engagement in silence by maintaining eye contact, adopting an open and receptive posture, and offering subtle nonverbal cues such as nodding or leaning in.

Express Gratitude

When the conversation concludes, make sure to also thank the person for trusting you with their thoughts and emotions. This simple expression of gratitude can reinforce the connection you've built during the conversation. It shows to the other person that you value the openness and vulnerability that they've shared with you.

Empathic Listening in Action

Empathic listening can be used in a wide array of situations ranging from personal relationships, professional settings, or even casual interactions. Here are a few examples of when empathic listening can be particularly valuable:

In Personal Relationships

Healthy relationships are vital for overall well-being as they provide emotional support, foster personal growth, and contribute to a sense of belonging and self-worth. And the cornerstone of it all is empathic listening.

Strengthening bonds with family and friends

One of the most rewarding aspects of this skill is its ability to strengthen the bonds you share with your loved ones. In this section, I will provide an overview of the various ways in which empathic listening can be employed to enhance connections with family and friends, ultimately nurturing and deepening these relationships.

Scenario 1: A friend sharing a difficult experience

Imagine your friend Sarah opens up to you about a recent breakup. She's devastated and unsure of how to move forward. Instead of offering unsolicited advice or jumping in with your own experiences, practice empathic listening by saying something like, "Sarah, it sounds like you're really hurting right now. Breakups can be so tough. I'm here for you."

In this response, you acknowledge her feelings, validate her experience, and offer support. This creates a safe space for Sarah to continue sharing her thoughts and emotions without feeling judged or dismissed.

Scenario 2: A family member grappling with a challenging decision

Envision your brother grappling with a difficult career decision, torn between accepting a high-paying job offer or pursuing his passion for art. As he shares his dilemma, practicing empathic listening can foster trust and connection. Instead of imposing your views on what he should do, you might say, "It sounds like you're facing a tough choice, and there's a lot at stake for you. I can understand why you're feeling conflicted. Can you tell me more about what you're considering?"

This response validates his emotions, demonstrates genuine interest in his thought process, and encourages him to explore his feelings further. Remember to refrain from giving unsolicited advice, and don't force your opinion on what to choose.

Navigating conflicts and misunderstandings

Empathic listening can also play a significant role in addressing conflicts and misunderstandings in our relationships. You can create a foundation for resolving issues and restoring harmony by demonstrating a genuine interest in understanding the other person's perspective,

Scenario 1: Miscommunication between friends

You and your friend, Mark, made plans to meet for dinner, but he arrived late, visibly upset. Instead of immediately expressing your frustration, you take a deep breath and try to understand Mark's situation. You ask him about his day, and he shares that he was stuck in a long, stressful meeting.

If you practice empathic listening, you can respond with, "Mark, it seems like your day was really challenging, and that meeting was tough. I understand why you're upset." Acknowledging and validating Mark's experience helps create an environment where he feels heard and understood, potentially preventing a larger conflict from arising.

Scenario 2: Family conflict resolution

Your sibling, Alex, and your parent have frequently been arguing, leading to a tense atmosphere at home. You decide to intervene and try to understand each person's perspective. You start by asking your sibling to share their thoughts while you practice empathic listening. You may say, "Alex, it sounds like you feel unheard and frustrated. I understand how that would be upsetting."

When you demonstrate empathy for Alex's emotions, you're encouraging open communication and helping to defuse the situation. You can then apply the same empathic listening skills with your parent, fostering understanding and resolving the conflict.

In the Workplace

Empathic listening plays a vital role in fostering a positive work environment and cultivating strong professional relationships. Maintaining these is essential for your growth and mental health at work. They can also foster mutual understanding and respect, boosting morale and productivity and ultimately contributing to your job satisfaction.

Enhancing Teamwork and Collaboration

Being attuned to the needs and emotions of your colleagues can help you to better support their ideas and contributions. Consider the scenarios below.

Scenario 1: Addressing a coworker's concerns

Your coworker, Emily, approaches you with concerns about her workload and the upcoming deadline for a project. Instead of brushing off her concerns, practice empathic listening by saying, "Emily, it sounds like you're feeling overwhelmed by the workload and the deadline. That must be really stressful for you."

In this response, you validate Emily's feelings and demonstrate your understanding of her concerns. By showing empathy, you create an environment where she feels heard and can discuss potential solutions.

Scenario 2: Collaborative problem-solving

During a team meeting, a disagreement arises over the allocation of resources for an upcoming project. You notice the discussion is heated, and you decide to step in and practice empathic listening.

You may tell one team member, "John, it sounds like you're concerned about ensuring we have enough resources dedicated to the project, and you feel strongly about your proposed allocation. Is that correct?" After receiving confirmation, you can turn to the other team member and explain, "And Susan, it seems like you're worried that allocating too many resources to this project might negatively impact other priorities. Is that accurate?" Acknowledging and validating each team member's perspective facilitates a more constructive conversation and encourages collaborative problem-solving.

Facilitating effective leadership and management

Leaders and managers can also utilize empathic listening, allowing them to build trust and rapport with their team, address concerns, and provide appropriate support. Consider the situation below.

Scenario 1: Providing feedback to an employee

You're a manager and need to provide feedback to an employee, David, who needs help with meeting deadlines. Instead of merely pointing out his shortcomings, practice empathic listening by saying, "David, I've noticed that you've been having difficulty meeting deadlines recently. It seems like you might be feeling overwhelmed or facing some challenges. Can you tell me more about what's going on?" This approach shows empathy and creates a safe space for David to share his concerns, allowing you to better understand and address the underlying issues.

Levelling up your company's customer service

In customer service roles across all industries, having excellent empathic listening skills is the rule, not the exception. As a service provider, you need to be able to figure out your customers' needs, empathize with their frustrations, and show genuine understanding to be able to address their concerns and serve them better. By utilizing this skill, you can build rapport, enhance satisfaction, and find effective solutions for them.

Scenario 1: Addressing a customer complaint

You work in customer service for an online retail company, and a customer reaches out with a complaint about receiving a damaged product. Instead of immediately offering a solution or dismissing the customer's concern, you practice empathic listening.

Customer: "I received the package today, but the item inside was damaged. I'm really disappointed."

You: "I'm so sorry to hear that. I understand how frustrating it must be to receive a damaged product when you were eagerly anticipating it. Thank you for bringing this to our attention."

Customer: "I was really looking forward to using it. Now I have to go through the hassle of returning it."

You: "I can imagine how inconvenient that is for you. It's important to us that you have a positive shopping experience, and I want to make this right for you. Could you please provide me with some details about the damage?"

By empathically listening and empathizing with the customer's disappointment and inconvenience, you're able to diffuse their frustration and take the necessary steps to rectify the situation.

In Mentoring and Coaching Successfully

Empathic listening is key to effective mentoring and coaching relationships. This understanding allows mentors to offer guidance, support, and feedback that is tailor-fit to their mentees' specific goals, challenges, and aspirations.

Scenario 1: Mentoring an overwhelmed young professional

You're a mentor who is working with a young professional who is feeling overwhelmed and unsure about their career path. Instead of immediately providing advice or solutions, you practice empathic listening to get to the root cause of their issue. You can practice saying, "I can understand how challenging and uncertain it must feel to be in this position. Exploring career paths and finding your passion can be overwhelming. Thank you for opening up to me about your concerns." Follow it up with "It's completely normal to have doubts and uncertainties along the way. Many professionals experience similar feelings at different stages of their career. Let's take some time to delve deeper into your interests, strengths, and goals. Understanding your unique strengths and values can help guide us in finding a path that aligns with your aspirations."

By actively listening and empathizing with the mentee's concerns, you acknowledge their feelings of confusion and offer reassurance. This approach creates a safe space for the mentee to express their worries openly and allows you to gain a better understanding of their needs. Through empathic listening, you can provide tailored guidance and support, helping the mentee gain clarity and confidence in their career journey.

Assessing and Refining Empathic Listening Skills

Mastering empathic listening is an ongoing journey of growth and self-improvement. To make the learning process more engaging and interesting, consider treating it as an exploration of human emotions and connections. After each conversation or interaction, take a moment to reflect on how well you practiced empathic listening. Ask yourself:

- Did I genuinely try hard to understand the other person's feelings and perspective?
- Did I acknowledge and validate their emotions without judgment?
- Did I refrain from interrupting or offering unsolicited advice?

You can pinpoint areas for growth and continue to enhance your empathic listening abilities in a dynamic and captivating way when you keep these questions in mind.

Consider actively seeking feedback from others to add another layer of excitement and depth to your empathic listening practice. I will discuss feedback more deeply in the third sub-book. For now, keep in mind that asking for feedback is a great way to hone your empathic listening skills.

After a conversation or interaction, you may ask the person you spoke with:

- Did you feel heard and understood during our conversation?
- Was there anything I could have done differently to better support or understand you?

This kind of feedback can provide a treasure trove of insights into how your empathic listening skills are perceived by others, enabling you to further refine and develop your abilities in a meaningful and impactful manner.

Skill-Building Activities

Exercise 1: Practicing Active Listening

Objective: Improve your active listening skills to better understand and empathize with others.

Instructions:

1. Pair up with a partner.
2. One person shares a recent experience while the other listens attentively.
3. The listener should practice the following active listening techniques:
4. Maintain eye contact.
5. Nod or use verbal cues (e.g., "Mhm," "I see")
6. Avoid interrupting or offering advice.
7. Paraphrase or summarize what the speaker said to confirm understanding.
8. Switch roles and repeat the exercise.

Exercise 2: Observing Empathic Listening

Objective: Learn from others' empathic listening skills by observing interactions in various settings.

Instructions:

1. Choose a public setting, such as a park, coffee shop, or online forum, where people interact and converse.
2. Observe at least two interactions while maintaining a respectful distance without intruding on their privacy.
3. Take notes on the empathic listening skills displayed, considering questions like:
4. "How did the listener show curiosity and interest?"
5. "What non-verbal cues did the listener use to convey empathy?"

6. "What types of questions did the listener ask to encourage deeper understanding?"
7. Reflect on the observations and identify techniques you can incorporate into your empathic listening practice.

Exercise 3: Imaginary Dialogues

Objective: Practice empathic listening in imagined scenarios to enhance skills in real-life situations.

Instructions:

1. Choose a fictional character or public figure you are familiar with.
2. Imagine a conversation between yourself and the selected person, focusing on a topic that might elicit strong emotions or opinions.
3. Write a dialogue, ensuring that your responses demonstrate empathic listening through open-ended questions, active listening, and non-judgmental responses.
4. Review the dialogue and consider areas where you could improve your empathic listening skills.

Self-Reflection Section

Spend 15 minutes reflecting on your experiences and progress with the previous exercises.

Consider the following questions:

1. What aspects of empathic listening did you find most challenging?
2. In what ways did empathic listening enhance your understanding of others' perspectives?
3. What improvements could you make in your empathic listening skills?

Create a personal action plan (I'll provide you with detailed steps on how to create an action plan in a later chapter) to continue developing your empathic listening skills, incorporating the insights gained during the exercises and self-reflection. Set specific goals and strategies for integrating empathic listening into your daily life, both in personal relationships and in professional settings.

Book 2

The Power of Inquiry

Mastering the Art of Asking the Right Questions for Improved Communication and Relationships

Table of Contents

Chapter 1: Foundations of Effective Questioning 55
Influence of Effective Questioning 56
Importance of Asking the Right Questions........................ 57
Elements of a Questioning Mindset 60
Critical Thinking in Inquiry 63

Chapter 2: Crafting Impactful Questions 65
Types of Questions 65
Techniques for Elaborating and Expanding
on Responses 68
Choosing a Questioning Approach 72
Exercises to Improve Questioning Skills 75

Chapter 3: Five Golden Tips of Questioning 79
1. Be Respectful and Polite 79
2. Get Creative 80
3. Be Mindful of the Timing and Delivery 81
4. Tailor Fit Questions Based on the Audience 83
5. Vulnerability, Authenticity, and
Openness in Conversations 85

Chapter 1:
Foundations of Effective Questioning

In a world where knowledge is abundant and readily available, your ability to ask questions becomes a valuable tool in navigating the complexities of life. The practice of inquiry allows you to foster a deeper understanding of the world, develop ties with others, and engage in more meaningful conversations. After practicing empathic listening, the natural progression is to ask insightful questions that further illuminate the topic. These two skills, empathic listening and thoughtful questioning are deeply intertwined. It forms the foundation for effective communication and strong interpersonal relationships.

As you listen intently to another person's experiences and viewpoints, you are better equipped to ask meaningful questions that encourage them to open up and share more about themselves. Asking questions enables you to gain new perspectives. It also challenges your assumptions, leading to personal growth and increased empathy for others. This dynamic process, similar to empathic listening, also creates an environment of trust and respect, fostering authentic connections and deepening our bonds with others.

Mastering these two essential communication skills is important. Through this, you can actively participate in conversations that enrich your understanding of the world and help to create a more compassionate, inclusive society. However, asking questions does not only nurture relationships but also promotes intellectual curiosity and fosters a lifelong love of learning.

After talking in detail about emphatic listening, in this chapter, I will now plunge into the art of asking questions. I will tackle its importance, benefits, and essential components so that you can be more effective in your questioning. I will talk about understanding the context of a conversation and adapting the questioning approach to suit it. To tie it all together, I will provide you with strategies for nurturing a questioning mindset.

Influence of Effective Questioning

The ability to ask questions impacts various facets of your life. When you actively engage with your environment through inquiry, you seek to make sense of the abundant information and experiences surrounding you. This process allows you to learn about the world through self-discovery. It changes the way you shape your thoughts, beliefs, and perspectives. Let me take you on a journey to explore the multifaceted importance of asking questions by examining its influence on cognitive development, problem-solving, decision-making, and self-awareness.

Cognitive Development

Asking questions plays a crucial role in cognitive development, or the process through which one's mental abilities evolve and mature. Studies have shown that children's ability to ask questions is closely linked to their intellectual growth and understanding of the world around them (Chin & Osborne, 2008). As children ask questions, they actively construct their knowledge, assimilate new information, and refine their understanding of various concepts. This process of inquiry lays the foundation for critical thinking, creativity, and lifelong learning.

Problem-Solving and Decision-Making

Research has demonstrated that individuals who ask questions during problem-solving tasks are more likely to generate creative and effective solutions (Graesser & Person, 1994). Questioning is vital in problem-solving and decision-making because it serves as a scalpel, dissecting complex issues into smaller, more digestible components. It helps you to better understand the problem, its causes, and possible solutions. This is because it guides you in collecting essential information systematically and enables you to assess the potential implications of each decision.

Self-Awareness and Personal Growth

Through inquiry, you also expand your understanding of both yourself and the world around you. You realize that the world is bigger than what you perceive and that there are a multitude of thoughts, beliefs, and perspectives that outright contradicts your own. Engaging in reflective questioning promotes introspection, allowing you to also recognize your strengths, weaknesses, and opportunities for growth.

Importance of Asking the Right Questions

The benefits of questioning are many, but the importance of posing the right questions cannot be overstated. Simply asking questions for the sake of inquiry is not enough. In this section, you'll see the significance of skillful questioning and its impact on communication. Uncover the transformative potential of well-crafted questions to also enhance your interactions and experiences.

It Enhances Communication and Understanding

Well-crafted, relevant questions can clarify complex ideas, uncover hidden assumptions, and reveal more profound insights. You foster mutual understanding and bridge gaps in knowledge or perspective when you focus on the most pertinent aspects of a conversation through the help of inquiry. Also, asking questions can help you identify any assumptions or misconceptions, thereby reducing misunderstandings and potential conflicts. It allows for the clarification of details, ensuring all parties have the same understanding, which is critical in communication.

Shows Interest and Engagement

Aside from being just a means to gather information, asking questions is a great way to show your interest and engagement in a conversation. By posing thoughtful questions, you show your conversation partners that you are actively listening. They'll sense that you're genuinely interested in understanding their perspectives and truly value their input. Research has shown that individuals who ask questions during social interactions are perceived as more likable, competent, and socially skilled, further emphasizing the importance of questions in effective communication (Huang et al., 2017). It's no wonder that authentic engagement makes others see you in a positive light.

Builds Negotiation Skills

By formulating well-considered questions, you can also significantly enhance your ability to negotiate and find common ground during conversations. It's a strategic approach to uncovering the needs, desires, and motivations of the other party.

When you ask the right questions, you can pinpoint underlying interests and objectives, which may otherwise remain hidden in the discourse. This understanding not only assists you in structuring your propositions more appealingly but also fosters empathy in the negotiation process. When you comprehend the perspective of your conversation partners, you can better appreciate their standpoint and approach the negotiation with more respect and consideration.

Understanding Context

Context plays a significant role in shaping your understanding of the information being shared. It dictates the meaning behind words, gestures, and expressions. When you fully grasp the context of what's being discussed, you can tailor fit your communication style, tone, and content to better align with the expectations and needs of your conversation partners. This helps you have a more engaging and productive dialogue, as it ensures that your responses resonate with the people you are conversing with, making the exchange more valuable. Asking the right questions helps with this.

Personally, it's quite challenging for me to pick up on subtle cues, especially at work. I remember being late to a team meeting, and as soon as I walked in, our team leader said, "It's getting heated over here, don't you guys think?" Of course, I didn't want to draw the attention to myself, so I turned the air conditioner and the fan on up to their highest setting to help cool the room. I proudly walked to my seat, only to see that my workmates were all staring at me while trying to keep themselves from laughing. At first, I was dumbfounded; then it dawned on me. The team leader was referring to the clashing ideas that the different departments were pitching. It was heated since the tone and content of the discussion were becoming intense and confrontational. I look back at this experience fondly as it's one of the many instances where I realized the importance of context in communication.

So, here's a piece of advice, don't make the same mistake as me! If you wish to truly understand the purpose and goals of an exchange, be sure ask questions first before deciding on what you're going to say or do. Make sure you are aware of the context.

Elements of a Questioning Mindset

Curiosity and inquisitiveness are some of the fundamentals in cultivating a questioning mindset. These two key elements, while having distinctive features, work together to motivate effective questioning.

Curiosity

Often described as a somewhat passive yet powerful motivation, curiosity kindles the urge to learn. Renowned psychologist George Loewenstein characterizes curiosity as a "cognitive itch" that arises when we encounter a gap in our knowledge. This recognition stimulates a motivation to fill it by seeking new information, experiences, and perspectives. Curious individuals possess a natural sense of wonder and openness to new experiences. Intrigued by the unknown, they are driven to explore unfamiliar territories purely for the pleasure of learning. In developing a questioning mindset, curiosity encourages you to remain open to new ideas, constantly question the status quo, and embrace a love for learning.

Inquisitiveness

This refers to the intentional act of seeking answers to our questions. It is a strong desire to acquire knowledge and understand various aspects of life, often by asking questions or conducting research. Inquisitive individuals are typically characterized by their relentless pursuit of answers and their propensity to engage in deep, probing questions. Inquisitiveness often manifests as a focused, goal-oriented approach to learning, where the individual is determined to gain specific insights or solve particular problems.

To illustrate this, consider a detective embodying inquisitiveness. She actively seeks evidence, poses targeted questions, and tirelessly investigates until she solves the case. Conversely, imagine an artist strolling through a gallery, captivated by diverse artworks without any specific objective other than experiencing the art and possibly finding inspiration.

Recognizing these nuances is crucial in developing a questioning mindset. While curiosity may spark the initial interest in a subject, inquisitiveness drives the pursuit of answers, maintaining momentum in the learning process. Inquisitiveness enables you to ask sharp questions, dig deeper, and persist until you gain clarity or resolution. This is why you have to first spark the curiosity within you and then maintain it by being inquisitive.

Together, curiosity and inquisitiveness empower you to approach conversations with an open and receptive mindset. Embracing this kind of attitude will bring your questioning skills to new heights.

Techniques for a Questioning Mindset

Cultivating a curious and inquisitive mindset requires ongoing practice and intentional effort. Here are some strategies to help you nurture curiosity and develop a questioning mindset:

- **Embrace Uncertainty:** Be comfortable with ambiguity and uncertainty, as it can open the door to new questions, ideas, and possibilities. Recognizing that there is often no single "right" answer can also inspire curiosity and encourage exploration.
- **Be Observant:** Practice observing the world around you with an open and curious mind. Pay attention to details, patterns, and connections that may have previously gone unnoticed, and use these observations as a springboard for asking questions.

- ***Seek Diverse Perspectives:*** Expose yourself to a wide range of ideas, cultures, and experiences to expand your understanding of the world. Engage with people who hold different viewpoints, read books or articles from various disciplines, and participate in activities that challenge your comfort zone. This exposure will stimulate your curiosity, inspire new questions, and help you develop a more comprehensive worldview.
- ***Practice Mindfulness:*** Mindfulness involves paying attention to the present moment with intention and non-judgment. By practicing mindfulness, you can cultivate greater self-awareness, recognize the gaps in your knowledge, and develop a deeper appreciation for the intricacies of the world around you. Incorporate mindfulness practices, such as meditation or journaling, into your daily routine to sharpen your curiosity and inquisitiveness.
- ***Be a Lifelong Learner:*** Commit to ongoing learning by setting personal and professional goals, attending workshops, taking online courses, or pursuing hobbies that challenge and excite you. Lifelong learning helps maintain a curious mindset, as it keeps your mind sharp and encourages you to continually seek new knowledge and experiences.
- ***Reflect on Your Own Questions:*** Regularly evaluate the questions you ask in conversations and interactions. Consider whether your questions are genuinely engaging, thought-provoking, and relevant to the topic at hand. Reflecting on your questioning habits will help you identify areas for improvement and hone your ability to ask meaningful questions.
- ***Explore New Subjects and Hobbies:*** Actively seek out new topics, disciplines, or hobbies that pique your interest. Diversifying your areas of interest can foster curiosity and encourage you to ask questions about various aspects of life.
- ***Engage in Creative Activities:*** Participate in activities that promote creativity, such as painting, writing, or playing

a musical instrument. Creative endeavors can stimulate your imagination and inspire curiosity about the world around you.
- ***Travel and Explore:*** Travel to new places, both locally and internationally, to immerse yourself in different cultures, environments, and experiences. Traveling can ignite your curiosity by exposing you to novel situations and broadening your perspectives.
- ***Surround Yourself with Curious People:*** Spend time with individuals who demonstrate a curious and inquisitive mindset, as their enthusiasm for learning and exploration can be contagious. Engage in conversations, activities, and projects with these individuals to foster a collaborative environment that encourages curiosity and questioning.
- ***Keep a Curiosity Journal:*** Dedicate a notebook or digital document to record your questions, observations, and insights. Regularly review your entries and track your progress in cultivating curiosity and inquisitiveness. This journal can serve as a valuable resource for sparking new ideas, identifying patterns in your thinking, and documenting your personal growth.

Critical Thinking in Inquiry

It's not enough to just ask questions and passively accept any answers that come your way. You must be critical and carefully analyze the responses you receive to discern their validity, relevance, and completeness. Critical thinking is akin to wearing a pair of analytical lenses that allow you to meticulously examine the answers you get. It involves questioning the question, so to speak. It involves understanding the "how" and "why" behind that information, allowing you to form a complete, well-rounded understanding of the subject at hand.

When you ask a question, remember that the answer you receive is often framed by the respondent's perspectives, biases, or knowledge limits. As such, it's crucial to remain critical and reflective when receiving them. Evaluate the response against what you already know, scrutinize the logic behind the answer, and don't hesitate to ask follow-up questions for clarification.

For instance, if someone makes a claim during a discussion, rather than taking it at face value, a critically minded individual might ask, "What evidence supports your claim?" or "Could you explain the rationale behind your argument?" These questions serve to dissect the information provided, ensuring it holds up to scrutiny and is backed by sound reasoning and evidence.

Being critical in asking questions will enable you to not only ask better but also to derive more value from the answers you receive. This is important since the real power of questions lies in how we interpret and act upon the answers we receive.

Chapter 2:
Crafting Impactful Questions

Have you ever found yourself struggling to get the information you need from a conversation? Perhaps you've asked a question and received a short, unhelpful response, or maybe you've struggled to keep a conversation focused and productive. Crafting impactful questions is a crucial skill for effective communication, whether conducting an interview, facilitating a discussion, or simply conversing with a friend or colleague. This chapter will explore techniques and strategies for improved inquiry skills by being familiar with the types of questions. You will see how these types have different goals and applications. Afterward, I'll guide you through formulating your own questions. I'll share with you tips on how you can identify what kind of questions to use depending on the situation. By the end of this chapter, you will have a toolkit of powerful questioning techniques that will enable you to facilitate productive and insightful conversations, even in challenging or complex situations.

Types of Questions

Open-ended and Closed-ended Questions

Understanding the difference between open-ended and closed-ended questions helps you to craft more effective and impactful queries. Each type of question serves a unique purpose and can lead to different outcomes in a conversation. When you recognize their characteristics and advantages, you can strategically utilize these questions to facilitate engaging discussions.

Open-ended questions are those that cannot be answered with a simple "yes" or "no." Instead, they require the person being asked to provide their thoughts, feelings, or opinions, leading to more in-depth and meaningful conversations. For example, "What did you think of the book?" or "How did you approach the project?"

Some common characteristics of open-ended questions include their ability to invite elaboration and personal insights, encourage creative thinking and problem-solving, and foster reflection and self-exploration. They are beneficial for building rapport and trust in relationships, encouraging critical thinking and self-awareness, and gaining a deeper understanding of a person's perspective or experiences. You can ask these questions when the goal is to explore a topic in-depth, gather diverse perspectives, or generate new ideas. They allow for a more detailed response and can encourage the respondent to share their thoughts and feelings.

On the other hand, closed-ended questions are designed to elicit specific, concise answers, often in the form of "yes" or "no." They typically begin with words like "did," "do," or "is." For example, "Did you like the book?" or "Is the project complete?"

They are useful when the goal is to obtain specific information quickly or keep the conversation focused. They allow for a more efficient exchange of information and can help to clarify details or confirm facts. Characteristics of closed-ended questions include their capacity to provide straightforward and definitive answers, help establish facts or clarify information, and allow for quick communication. Asking these offers benefits such as facilitating decision-making and problem-solving, structuring conversations and guiding discussions, and assessing knowledge or comprehension.

The choice between open-ended and closed-ended questions depends on the situation and the goals of the conversation. The former best suits situations where you want to delve deeper into someone's thoughts, feelings, and experiences. While the latter is more appropriate when seeking specific facts or details.

The most effective questioning involves a balance of both open-ended and closed-ended questions. By using both types of questions, the conversation can move fluidly between exploring a topic in-depth and obtaining specific information. It can lead to a more productive discussion and a better understanding of the topic at hand. Here are some tips for achieving that balance:

- ***Assess the situation and context***: Different situations call for different types of questions.
- ***Consider the desired outcome:*** Reflect on the information or insights you hope to gain from the conversation. Open-ended questions are more suitable if you're seeking to understand someone's feelings or opinions. Conversely, closed-ended questions are the way to go if you need specific facts or details.
- ***Use both types:*** As the conversation progresses, you may need to switch between open-ended and closed-ended questions based on the responses you receive. Be prepared to adapt your questioning style to keep the conversation flowing and achieve your objectives. For example, let's say you are conducting an interview with a job candidate. You might start with open-ended questions to allow the candidate to provide a detailed response about their background and experience. It can help you understand their qualifications and gauge how fit they are for the position. As the interview progresses, you may switch to closed-ended questions to obtain specific information about their skills and experience, such as "Have you managed a team before?" or "Are you familiar with XYZ software?"

Probing Questions

Probing questions are a powerful tool for encouraging the elaboration and exploration of ideas. These are like open-ended questions as they both play a crucial role in eliciting more in-depth responses and fostering the exploration of ideas. The difference though is while open-ended questions are designed to initiate broader discussions and enable respondents to express their thoughts freely, probing questions serve a more specific purpose: to clarify, expand upon, or delve deeper into the respondent's previous answer.

For example, an open-ended question may be, "What did you think of the book?" a probing follow-up could be, "Can you talk more about why you found the protagonist's journey compelling?" This pinpoints a specific aspect of the original response, pressing for more depth and clarity. You can also see that probing questions dig deeper into the layers of conversation, uncovering insights that might not have surfaced with open-ended questions alone.

Techniques for Elaborating and Expanding on Responses

Probing questions can unlock new realms of conversation. It enables you to tap into the deeper recesses of thought and inspire others to expand upon their initial ideas. It's about sparking intellectual curiosity, encouraging the exploration of alternative perspectives, and drawing out the hidden potential in each conversation. These strategies will enable you to extract more meaningful and in-depth information from the person you're speaking with.

- ***Building on their response:*** Listen attentively to the person's answer and build upon it by asking follow-up questions or making connections to their statement. You can also encourage the person to provide specific examples or situations that illustrate their point.
- ***Encouraging reflection:*** Prompt the person to think more deeply about their response and consider different aspects of the topic. An example would be, "How do you think your preference for teamwork has influenced your career choices and job satisfaction?"

- ***Validating their perspective:*** Show understanding and appreciation for their viewpoint, even if you don't necessarily agree. This validation can encourage them to explore their thoughts further. You can do this by echoing wherein it involves repeating part of the respondent's answer and asking for further clarification or elaboration. Restating is another technique where you rephrase the respondent's answer and ask for confirmation or additional information.
- ***Seeking clarification***: If you're unsure about the meaning of a response, don't be afraid to ask the respondent to explain further or clarify their statement.

Socratic Questions

Socratic questioning is a distinctive and potent technique that differs from the types of questions mentioned before. Characterized by its focus on challenging assumptions and beliefs, Socratic questioning promotes critical thinking and a more profound understanding of a subject. This method is versatile and can be applied in various settings, from educational to professional contexts. The approach distinguishes itself by targeting an argument's or perspective's logic rather than merely eliciting broader thoughts or probing deeper into existing ones. This unique angle helps reveal potential weaknesses in reasoning and stimulates the exploration of fresh viewpoints by challenging individuals with inquiries that shake up their habitual thought processes.

This method of inquiry, derived from the teachings of the ancient Greek philosopher Socrates, encourages you to scrutinize the basis of your beliefs and assumptions.

To be able to use it effectively, you must first understand and internalize its core principles. They are:

- ***Examine assumptions and consider alternative perspectives:*** These are questions that encourage the respondent

to explore the underlying assumptions that shape their beliefs or opinions. Then it invites them to consider different viewpoints or possibilities.
- **Assess evidence and reasoning:** Socratic questions challenge the respondents to support their answers by providing evidence or justification for their beliefs or opinions.
- **Explore implications and consequences:** These questions prompt respondents to contemplate the potential outcomes or repercussions stemming from their beliefs or decisions. Through introspection, they may engage in a healthy self-examination, leading to a deeper understanding of their standpoints, the validity of their beliefs, or the potential impacts of their choices. Rather than promoting doubt, this process fosters a critical self-awareness that can be enlightening and constructive.

To illustrate, let's take the context of a business strategy meeting. An executive has just proposed a new marketing plan, firmly stating, "I believe we should focus all our marketing efforts online because traditional marketing is dead."

If you want to apply the principle of examining assumptions in this scenario, you could ask: "Can you help me understand the basis of your belief that traditional marketing has lost its relevance?" This question requests the executive to unravel the underlying assumptions informing their viewpoint.

Next, to stimulate consideration of alternative perspectives, you could propose: "Could there still be certain demographic groups or market segments that engage better with traditional marketing? Could employing a hybrid strategy of online and traditional marketing increase our reach?"

Finally, to explore implications and consequences, pose the question: "If we direct all our efforts toward online marketing, what might be the potential impact on our traditional customer base?

Could this shift result in us overlooking some segments of our target market?"

These questions not only inspire the executive to reassess their original assumption but also facilitate the discussion towards alternative viewpoints, exploring possible ramifications. The result could be a more holistic and inclusive marketing strategy that benefits from both online engagement and traditional outreach.

Applications in Various Contexts

Socratic questioning can be applied in a wide range of settings, making it a versatile and powerful tool for deepening understanding and fostering critical thinking. Here are some engaging examples:

In a dynamic classroom setting, an innovative teacher may use Socratic questioning to ignite lively debates and stimulate critical thinking. It challenges students to question their assumptions about a particular topic and enables the teacher to foster an atmosphere of intellectual curiosity and growth. Students can also develop a deeper appreciation for the complexities of the subject matter when they employ this questioning.

Within the transformative space of coaching or therapy, a skilled practitioner may utilize Socratic questioning to help clients unravel their beliefs, values, and motivations. Prompting clients to examine their assumptions and explore alternative perspectives can benefit them. The practitioner empowers them to gain self-awareness, recognize potential blind spots, and make more informed life decisions.

In the realm of everyday conversations, individuals can benefit from incorporating Socratic questioning techniques into interactions. Whether it's a friendly debate at a dinner party or a challenging discussion with a colleague, it allows the discovery of each other's intricate perspectives.

Formulating Effective Questions

Knowing which type of question to ask can make or break a conversation. It's all about reading the room and knowing what you're aiming to achieve when you talk to people. It may seem simple, but it's actually challenging to form effective questions that can elevate your conversations. Below are some strategies that can help you determine the type of question suitable for a particular situation and formulate the actual questions.

- **Determine your goal:** Before formulating a question, identify the purpose of your inquiry. Are you looking to gather specific information, explore a topic more deeply, or challenge someone's assumptions? Your goal will help guide your choice of question type.
- **Keep it simple and straightforward:** Aim for simplicity and clarity regardless of your question type. Ensure your question is easy to understand and avoids ambiguity, which can lead to confusion and misunderstandings.
- **Consider the context:** The context of your conversation will play a significant role in determining the most appropriate type of question to ask.

Choosing a Questioning Approach

The key to effective questioning lies in understanding which type of question best suits a given situation. Once you have identified the purpose and goals of a conversation, you must tailor your questioning approach based on the conversation's context. Here are some examples:

- *Casual Conversations:* In informal settings, opt for lighthearted questions to encourage easygoing, free-flowing discussions. This approach helps establish rapport and fosters a relaxed, comfortable atmosphere.

- ***Professional Discussions:*** For workplace or professional discourse, focus on specific, goal-oriented questions addressing the task. This method ensures the conversation remains productive and on-topic.
- ***Sensitive Topics:*** When discussing sensitive or emotionally charged subjects, choose empathetic and supportive questions demonstrating understanding and respect for the other person's feelings. It is essential to approach these conversations with tact and a genuine willingness to listen.
- ***Learning and Growth:*** In educational or growth-oriented discourse, aim for thought-provoking questions that stimulate critical thinking, reflection, and deeper understanding. This approach encourages exploration and the expansion of knowledge.

When you comprehend the context of a conversation and adjust your questioning technique accordingly, you guarantee that your inquiries are suitable to the discussion and that it contributes to meaningful engagement.

Here are a series of scenarios that illustrate when to choose open-ended, closed-ended, Socratic, or probing questions, ensuring that your conversations are engaging, insightful, and productive.

Building rapport and fostering connection

Open-ended questions are your best choice if you're meeting someone new and want to create a strong connection.

Example: "What inspired you to choose your current career path?"

The question not only demonstrates your interest in the person's journey, but also provides insights into their passions, aspirations, and personal history. It opens the door to exploring various facets of their life in a non-intrusive manner. To go deeper into the conversation, you can follow up with, "What drove you to pursue your career – was it a long-standing hobby, a sudden spark of interest, or a different factor entirely?"

Gathering specific information in a time-sensitive situation

When you need to quickly collect precise information, closed-ended questions are ideal. These questions are perfect for confirming details, gathering facts, and guiding the direction of a conversation.

Example: "Did the project meet the deadline?"

Such a question will fetch you a straightforward answer, offering the critical information you seek without superfluous details. It enables you to quickly ascertain the state of affairs and make timely decisions, making it an indispensable tool in fast-paced or data-driven environments.

Engaging in a lively debate or intellectual discussion

Socratic questioning is particularly useful in debates, as it compels participants to consider alternative viewpoints, thereby broadening their understanding of the issue at hand. This, in turn, fosters a more comprehensive and balanced discussion.

Example: "How do you think your opinion would change if you considered the opposing argument?"

By asking this, you invite the respondent to step into the shoes of the opposition, helping them to see the issue from a different angle. It encourages a holistic examination as it illuminates otherwise overlooked perspectives, enriching the overall discourse.

Clarifying a statement during a negotiation or conflict resolution

When you're involved in a negotiation or conflict resolution, and you need to dig deeper into a response to clarify someone's statements or encourage further elaboration, probing questions are the most suitable choice.

Example: "Can you explain what you meant when you said the proposal was unfair?"

The question tries to expand on the respondent's viewpoint. It opens the door to deeper understanding, facilitates mutual empathy, and propels the conversation toward resolution. It's a critical instrument for managing disagreements and fostering constructive dialogue.

Keep in mind that crafting effective questions is not a one-size-fits-all process. Instead, it requires careful consideration of your inquiry's goals, context, and desired outcome. Through practice and experience, you can become more proficient at crafting impactful questions that can help you become a better listener.

Exercises to Improve Questioning Skills

Ready to level up your questioning skills? The following exercises and activities are designed to help you practice and refine your ability to craft open-ended, closed-ended, and Socratic questions. By engaging with these fun and interactive exercises, you'll sharpen your questioning abilities and enhance your communication skills.

Question Transformation Challenge

In this exercise, you'll practice transforming different types of questions into their alternative forms.

Instructions:

1. Find a list of questions or come up with your own (aim for at least 10).
2. For each question, identify whether it is open-ended, closed-ended, or Socratic.
3. Rewrite the question in a different form (e.g., turn an open-ended question into a closed-ended question or a Socratic question).

Example:

1. Original question: "Do you enjoy reading?" (Closed-ended)
2. Transformed question: "What do you enjoy most about reading?" (open-ended) or "Why do you think reading is an important activity?" (Socratic)

The Question Relay

This activity is best done with a partner or a small group. It's a great way to practice crafting questions on the spot and encourages active listening.

Instructions:

1. Choose a topic or let the first person in the group choose one.
2. The first person asks a question related to the topic.
3. The next person answers the question and then asks a new question based on the previous answer.
4. Continue the relay, with each person answering the previous question and asking a new one.
5. Aim to incorporate a mix of open-ended, closed-ended, and Socratic questions in the relay.

Socratic Dialogue Role-Play

Engage in a role-play exercise with a partner to practice Socratic questioning techniques. This activity can help you become more comfortable with challenging assumptions and beliefs through your questions.

Instructions:

1. Choose a topic or issue that has room for debate.
2. One person takes on the role of Socrates, asking questions that encourage the other person to clarify their stance, explore assumptions, and consider alternative perspectives.
3. The other person responds to the questions, reflecting on their beliefs and ideas.
4. Switch roles after 10-15 minutes.

Questioning Journal

Maintaining a questioning journal is an excellent way to reflect on your questioning skills and track your progress over time.

Instructions:

1. Dedicate a notebook or digital document to your questioning journal.
2. Each day, jot down at least one open-ended, closed-ended, and Socratic question related to your daily experiences, conversations, or observations.
3. Reflect on how the different types of questions might lead to different outcomes or insights.

The 5 Whys Exercise

The 5 Whys is a simple yet powerful technique to practice asking probing questions and uncovering the root cause of an issue. This exercise can be done individually or with a partner.

Instructions:

1. Identify a problem or issue you'd like to explore.
2. Ask "Why?" in response to the problem, seeking an explanation.
3. For each subsequent answer, ask "Why?" again, digging deeper into the issue.
4. Continue asking "Why?" until you've reached five levels of inquiry.
5. Reflect on the insights you've gained through this process and how the different types of questions (open-ended, closed-ended, Socratic) might be incorporated into the 5 Whys exercise.

By regularly practicing these exercises and activities, you'll build your questioning skills and enhance your ability to craft impactful open-ended, closed-ended, and Socratic questions. Remember, practice makes perfect! The more you engage with these exercises, the more natural and effective your questioning abilities will become.

Chapter 3:
Five Golden Tips of Questioning

My journey to becoming a more effective listener has been filled with years of trials and errors. What helped a lot were strategies that guided me on how to formulate thought-provoking questions. In this chapter, I'll share those techniques with you. It can be simplified to the Five Golden Tips of Questioning. I have found these to be incredibly helpful in my own conversations and have used them repeatedly. Let's explore each of these golden rules in-depth to give you a clear idea of how to implement these strategies in your own conversations.

1. Be Respectful and Polite

Alright, let's talk about something incredibly important when it comes to asking questions: being respectful and polite. I know, I know – it may seem like common sense, but trust me, it's worth taking a moment to really think about how you're asking your questions. I've learned that when I'm genuinely respectful and polite in my approach, I not only make people feel more at ease but also create the foundation for deeper, more meaningful conversations.

Being respectful and polite in your questioning is like having a secret key that unlocks the treasure chest of deeper conversations. When you approach someone with genuine curiosity, politeness, and respect, they're more likely to discuss and share their thoughts and feelings with you. For example, there was a time when I was chatting with a new acquaintance at a social event. Instead of bombarding them with a series of rapid-fire questions, I decided to take a more respectful and polite approach. I started by saying, "Hey, I'm really curious about your thoughts on this topic, but I don't want to put you on the spot. Feel free to share as much or as little as you'd like." This simple gesture of respect made them feel more at ease which resulted to them being comfortable enough to share their thoughts and opinions with me.

When it comes to being respectful and polite in your questioning, just remember the golden rule: treat others as you'd like to be treated. It's really that simple! Put yourself in their shoes and consider how you would feel if someone asked you the same question. This empathetic approach will help you connect with others on a deeper level and make your conversations more engaging and enjoyable for everyone involved.

2. Get Creative

We've all experienced that awkward moment when a conversation starts to fizzle out, and we're desperately grasping on to any thread of discussion, trying to keep it alive. I can totally relate to this struggle. My brain often craves stimulation, and if the conversation isn't engaging, I easily lose focus. But fear not, as I've discovered that asking the right questions is like throwing a lifeline to a sinking chat.

Take, for example, a time when I found myself at a friend's birthday party where I barely knew anyone. I knew I had to avoid the usual "So, what do you do for a living?" and try something different. So, I decided to go with, "What's something you're really passionate about?" Let me tell you, the response was nothing short of amazing! People began going into details about their hobbies, interests, and even some of their wildest dreams. The conversations that unfolded were so much deeper and more engaging, all because I switched up my questioning strategy.

Believe me, I've found that embracing this fearlessness in asking questions has made all the difference in keeping my focus and making genuine connections with others. Make sure to go out of the box and try to think of creative questions. These often involve hypothetical scenarios, abstract concepts, or inquiries that require people to tap into their imagination or personal experiences. They promote critical thinking and stimulate curiosity, making the conversation lively and stimulating. They can also serve as ice-breakers in a conversation, transforming a mundane or awkward conversation into an enjoyable and memorable interaction.

From a listener's perspective, creative questions can be exciting and refreshing. They can break the monotony of predictable conversations and bring a sense of fun and exploration. It also signals that you're interested in more than just superficial talk and is genuinely interested in understanding their perspective or hearing their stories.

Moreover, creative questions can enhance the depth and quality of a conversation. They encourage people to reflect more profoundly and express thoughts that they might not typically share.

Don't be afraid to switch up your questions or ask something a little out of the ordinary. As long as you approach the conversation with genuine curiosity, politeness, and respect, you'll be surprised at how receptive people can be.

3. Be Mindful of the Timing and Delivery

Let's dive a little deeper into one that I find particularly important: taking note of timing and delivery when asking questions. As someone with ADHD, I know how tempting it can be to blurt out a question the second it pops into my head. I find that refining this element of communication requires conscious effort. You would need to develop self-control and exercise patience and thoughtfulness before launching your inquiries.

Paying attention to timing means being aware of the natural flow of conversation and looking for those perfect moments to ask your thought-provoking questions. Similar to empathic listening, you should avoid interruptions. We've all been in those situations where someone asks a question that feels completely out of place or interrupts the flow of conversation. Don't be that person! Instead, try to listen carefully and wait for the right moment to jump in with your question.

For instance, I was at a dinner party a while back and found myself in a fascinating conversation about traveling. I had a burning question about the challenges of long-term travel, but my friend was still talking about the beautiful sites she visited. Instead of blurting it out, I waited for a lull in the conversation. When the moment arrived, I asked my question, leading to a fascinating discussion. It benefited us both as I got to have my question answered while my friend was able to share her experiences with our friends, who were also closely listening.

How you ask something can often be just as important as what you're asking. Tone, body language, and the words you choose can all play a role in how your question is received. Think about empathic listening for a moment. You learned that when you listen with empathy, you're not just hearing the words someone is saying; you're also paying attention to their tone, body language, and emotions. The same principle applies to asking questions. When you are mindful of how your question will be received, you can avoid misunderstandings and create a more supportive environment for conversation.

One time, I found myself in a deep conversation with a friend who was going through a challenging time in their life. I knew that the way I asked could make all the difference. If not careful, they might interpret my tone as sarcastic, as if I were criticizing or blaming them. Thus, I chose to approach the situation with genuine care and empathy. Rather than simply asking, "What's wrong with you?" which could come across as accusatory or insensitive, I gently inquired, "I've noticed you seem a bit overwhelmed lately. Is there anything you'd like to talk about or share?" This empathetic approach allowed my friend to feel comfortable enough to tell me about their struggles.

So, how can you practice better timing and delivery in your questioning? Here are a few more tips I've found helpful:

- *Be patient:* Resist the urge to blurt out your questions as soon as they come to mind. Wait for the right moment while focusing on what the other person is saying. Look for natural pauses or transitions to ask your questions.
- *Adjust your tone:* Make sure your tone matches the context of the conversation. A playful, lighthearted question might call for a more upbeat tone, while a sensitive topic may require a softer, more empathetic approach.
- *Be mindful of body language:* Your body language can also send a powerful message. Maintain eye contact, lean in slightly, and use open gestures to show that you're genuinely interested and engaged.

4. Tailor Fit Questions Based on the Audience

Just like how you adjust your clothing depending on the weather or occasion, adapting your questions to suit the person you're talking to can make your conversations more engaging, relevant, and enjoyable. I've found that this practice also helps me stay focused and connected during conversations.

Understanding Your Conversation Partner

The first step in tailoring your questions is understanding the person you're talking to. What are their interests? What's their background? What might they be comfortable discussing? By taking the time to learn more about your conversation partner, you can ask questions that resonate with them on a deeper level. For example, let me share an incident from a social gathering I attended a few years back.

At the event, I met Tom, a recently retired military veteran. Knowing his background, one might be tempted to ask about his time in the military, perhaps to satisfy a curiosity about his experiences or insights. However, it's crucial to remember that not all topics are comfortable for everyone, and certain experiences, particularly traumatic ones, may be sensitive areas.

Having prior knowledge about the psychological effects many veterans face, I decided to tread lightly on the topic of his military service. Instead, I asked, "Tom, now that you've embarked on this new chapter post-retirement, what are some hobbies or interests you're excited to explore?"

In doing so, I respected Tom's boundaries and focused on his future aspirations, a topic that would likely be more comfortable and enjoyable for him to discuss. My approach demonstrated an understanding of his background, as well as consideration for potentially sensitive topics.

Adjusting According to the Pace of Conversation

One of the challenges when engaging in conversations is that our minds can sometimes jump from one topic to another at lightning speed. While this can make discussions exciting and dynamic, it's important to remember that not everyone processes information or engages in conversation at the same pace. That's why you must adjust your questions to suit the rhythm and flow of the conversation. Take into account the individual communication styles of those you're conferring with.

Even when you're talking to someone you've just met or don't know well, there are still ways to tailor your questions effectively. Here's how:

- **Use Observational Insights:** When you lack prior knowledge about someone, the surroundings or the situation can offer cues. The context in which you're interacting, their body language, tone of voice, or even their attire can pro-

vide insights. For instance, if you're at a book club meeting and notice a newcomer holding a science fiction novel, you might start with, "That's one of my favorite genres. Which other science fiction authors do you enjoy?"
- **Have Respectful Curiosity:** When talking to strangers, your questions should be driven by genuine curiosity but also by respect for their comfort and privacy. Avoid potentially sensitive topics unless they steer the conversation there. You can use non-invasive personal questions that show your interest in them without crossing boundaries.
- **Find Shared Experiences or Interests:** Identify any common ground between you and the person you're talking to. This could be anything from a shared hobby, profession, interest, or even the event you're both attending.

5. Vulnerability, Authenticity, and Openness in Conversations

Let's now explore another aspect that I believe is needed for creating meaningful connections: being open, vulnerable, and authentic. Now, I know that it may be uncomfortable when it feels like we're wearing our hearts on our sleeves. But in my experience, embracing our true selves and being willing to share our thoughts and feelings can lead to some of the most rewarding conversations of our lives.

The Effect of Vulnerability

When you allow yourself to be vulnerable in conversations, you're opening the door for more profound connections with others. By sharing your own experiences, emotions, and even fears, you're inviting the other person to do the same – and that's where the magic happens. I remember a conversation I had with an acquaintance about our struggles with mental health. By deciding to bare my experiences with ADHD and the challenges I've faced along the way, I encouraged them to share their own journey with anxiety. This vulnerable exchange not only brought us closer together but also allowed us to support and learn from one another.

Authenticity in Questioning

Asking questions from a place of authenticity means genuinely wanting to know the other person's thoughts, feelings, and experiences. Avoid posing questions to which you already know the answers, as this can sound patronizing and can make others feel inferior. Instead, approach the questioning process with authenticity and genuine curiosity. Demonstrate your eagerness to learn and seek answers to the truly perplexing inquiries on your mind. For instance, during a group discussion about environmental conservation, you may already know the benefits of reducing single-use plastics. Rather than asking, "Don't you think reducing single-use plastics is beneficial for the environment?" – a question that might make others feel as if they are being tested or judged – opt for a more genuine inquiry, such as, "What other ways can we implement to minimize our environmental impact aside from reducing single-use plastics?" Remember, the goal of questioning isn't to show off your knowledge or put others in a tight spot but rather to encourage the exchange of ideas.

Openness to Responses

The thing to remember about questioning is that it comes with an essential responsibility. And that is being open to whatever answers that may come your way. Every question you pose opens a door that allows you to access diverse perspectives, often shedding light on facets you might not have considered before. This openness requires not just an intellectually receptive mind but also an empathetic heart that respects the varied lived experiences that shape each other's beliefs. Being open-minded allows you to navigate these multitudes of perspectives. It also shows respect, prompting people to share their thoughts freely and authentically. As we encourage others to voice their own viewpoints, we move a step closer to embracing the complexity of human experiences.

Book 3

Feedback Mastery

The Art of Giving and Receiving Constructive
Feedback for Personal and Professional Growth

Book 3

Feedback Mastery

The Art of Giving and Receiving Constructive
Feedback in To-guided by Raymond Lowell

Table of Contents

Chapter 1: The Basics of Feedback **91**
    Benefits of Feedback 91
    Five Types of Feedback 93
    The Interplay of Giving and Receiving Feedback 96

Chapter 2: Giving Feedback **101**
    The SBI Model 103

Chapter 3: Receiving Feedback **117**
    Growth Mindset in Relation to Feedback 117
    Challenges in Receiving Feedback 118
    Asking for Feedback Effectively 121
    Turning Feedback into Action 123

Chapter 1:
The Basics of Feedback

Bill Gates once said, "We all need people who will give us feedback. That's how we improve." He couldn't have been more right! Feedback is an essential component of our growth. It's like receiving a GPS signal when you've taken a wrong turn; it helps you find your way back to the right path.

In this chapter, we'll talk about the benefits of feedback. We'll explore its five types, according to renowned psychologist Carl Rogers, diving into each type and its unique applications in different contexts. We'll look into the power of feedback for personal and professional development as we navigate the art of giving and receiving feedback effectively. Together, we'll unravel the critical factors that contribute to a smooth feedback process for both the giver and receiver.

Benefits of Feedback

When wielded with skill and grace, feedback has the potential to act as a driving force for change. It's like watering a plant, providing the essential nourishment needed for growth and development. It can help you in various ways.

You can Identify your strengths and weaknesses. Feedback sheds light on your areas of expertise as well as where you need improvement. It's like holding up a mirror, helping you see yourself more clearly and objectively. It encourages self-reflection and introspection, allowing you to better understand your actions, behaviors, and impact on others. Because of this, it is important that you don't look at feedback as something negative but rather think of it as a compass that gives you a sense of purpose and direction. Through this, you can capitalize on your talents and develop strategies to overcome challenges.

Feedback builds trust, respect, and rapport. When you engage in open, honest, and supportive feedback exchanges, you create an environment of mutual respect where people feel valued, heard, and understood. This fosters stronger connections and promotes teamwork, ultimately contributing to a more positive and productive atmosphere.

It motivates you. Receiving recognition and appreciation for your hard work can ignite motivation and increase job satisfaction. When you celebrate your achievements and acknowledge your progress, you feel more engaged and committed to your goals. Remember, feedback is an ongoing process that promotes learning, growth, and development. With each piece of feedback received, you gain new insights and knowledge, empowering you to adapt, evolve, and flourish in both your personal and professional lives.

It cultivates innovation and creativity. Feedback encourages you to develop innovative thinking. It challenges you to generate different and new ideas. By receiving feedback that values and encourages your creativity, you feel empowered to think outside the box, take risks, and explore new approaches. Feedback can nurture a culture of innovation within organizations and stimulate continuous improvement.

It helps with performance evaluation. Feedback can be a helpful tool when conducting performance evaluation and measurement. It provides an opportunity to assess progress, measure outcomes, and identify areas where individuals or teams may require additional support or resources. By providing feedback, organizations can ensure that performance aligns with goals and objectives.

Promotes continuous learning. Feedback promotes a culture of nonstop learning and development. It encourages you to seek feedback, reflect on your experiences, and embrace a growth mindset. Through ongoing feedback, you can continuously adapt, learn from their mistakes, and evolve your skills and knowledge.

Five Types of Feedback

According to the renowned psychologist Carl Rogers, there are five distinct types of feedback that can be used in various situations to facilitate self-awareness, learning, and improvement. Here is an in-depth guide for you to better understand these five feedback types and their applications in different contexts.

1. Evaluative Feedback

Evaluative feedback involves making judgments or assessments of a person's performance, behavior, or attitude. While it can provide valuable information into areas of improvement, it may sometimes be perceived as critical or threatening for the receiver. Therefore, you, as the giver, should approach this type of feedback with sensitivity and care, ensuring that the focus remains on growth and development rather than criticism.

This type of feedback is commonly used in formal settings such as performance reviews or academic evaluations. To better illustrate this, here are some examples:

- *Performance reviews:* Managers can use evaluative feedback to assess employees' performance against predefined goals and objectives, identifying areas of strength and weaknesses.
- *Academic evaluations:* Teachers and professors can use evaluative feedback to grade students' work, providing insight into their understanding of the subject matter and areas where they may need further support.

- **Athletic coaching:** Coaches can use evaluative feedback to assess athletes' performance, identifying areas where they excel and where they need to focus on improvement.

2. Interpretive Feedback

Interpretive feedback is usually used to request confirmation or clarification of a message. Receiving this kind of feedback encourages the receiver to communicate more explicitly and be clearer. Do not be afraid to give interpretive feedback since it's always useful to verify your understanding. Additionally, this practice can often be viewed as a compliment, as it demonstrates your genuine interest in the speaker's words.

Interpretive feedback is used in situations where the message is confusing or hard to understand and needs additional clarification. Some examples include:

- **Journalistic Interviews:** Journalists often use interpretive feedback to get a clearer picture of their interviewee's opinions.
- **Conflict resolution:** In situations where disagreements or misunderstandings arise, interpretive feedback can help individuals gain a better understanding of each other's perspectives, fostering empathy and mutual understanding.
- **Creative collaboration:** Interpretive feedback can help individuals in artistic or creative settings to explore different ideas and interpretations, fostering innovation and originality.

3. Supportive Feedback

Supportive feedback focuses on providing encouragement, validation, and emotional support to the recipient. It is often used to boost morale, build self-esteem, and cultivate a sense of belonging. It can be particularly powerful in helping individuals overcome challenges, maintain motivation, and develop resilience in the face of adversity.

Supportive feedback plays an important role in numerous situations where affirmation and motivation are necessary. Some examples include:

- ***Personal relationships:*** Friends, family members, and romantic partners can use supportive feedback to express appreciation, validate each other's feelings, and provide reassurance during challenging times.
- ***Mentorship:*** Mentors can use supportive feedback to motivate and inspire their mentees, helping them build self-confidence and overcome obstacles.
- ***Team dynamics:*** In team settings, supportive feedback can foster a sense of belonging and camaraderie, promoting teamwork and collaboration.

4. Probing Feedback

Probing feedback involves asking questions that encourage the recipient to explore their thoughts, feelings, and actions more deeply. It allows the recipient to take ownership of their learning and growth by asking questions. This encourages a sense of autonomy and empowerment.

Probing feedback is most effective in situations that require self-reflection, critical thinking, and problem-solving. Some examples include:

- ***Coaching sessions:*** Life and career coaches can use probing feedback to encourage clients to explore their thoughts, feelings, and actions more deeply, fostering self-discovery and personal growth.
- ***Brainstorming sessions:*** In group discussions or meetings, probing feedback can stimulate deeper thinking and spark new ideas or solutions.

- *Personal growth:* Individuals can use probing feedback to reflect on their experiences and behaviors, promoting self-awareness and personal development.

5. Directive Feedback

Directive feedback involves giving specific instructions, guidance, or advice to help someone learn and grow. It is effective, but bear in mind that you need to use it wisely. Providing too much direction might unintentionally diminish the person's sense of independence and confidence in their abilities.

It is useful in situations where the recipient requires clear direction or assistance in accomplishing a task or overcoming a challenge. Here are some examples for you to better differentiate it from other types:

- *Skills development:* In educational or professional settings, directive feedback can help individuals learn new skills, techniques, or strategies.
- *Problem-solving:* When faced with complex problems or challenges, directive feedback can provide clear direction and guidance on how to proceed.
- *Project management:* In project-based work, directive feedback can help team members stay on track, ensuring that tasks are completed efficiently and effectively.

The Interplay of Giving and Receiving Feedback

Regardless of the type of feedback being used, it is essential to recognize the dynamic interplay between the giver and receiver of feedback. Both parties have a role that they play in the feedback process, with the giver responsible for delivering feedback in a clear, empathic, and constructive manner, and the receiver responsible for being open, receptive, and willing to learn from the feedback provided. Understanding the nuances of each feedback type allows both to adapt their approach and communication style accordingly. This ensures that feedback is delivered and received in the most effective and impactful way possible.

Cultivate a Feedback Culture

Establishing a culture that values feedback is fundamental for having healthy communication in both personal and professional settings. This means creating an environment where feedback is not only accepted but also valued and actively sought after. When feedback is seen as a valuable resource for learning and growth, individuals and organizations are more likely to embrace it as an opportunity for self-reflection and improvement. By encouraging the exchange of feedback, both positive and constructive, a culture of continuous learning and development can thrive. It is similar to the environment of trust I tackled in the past chapters. Both encourage open communication, mutual support, and shared learning. However, feedback culture is different as it is an environment where individuals feel empowered to take risks, learn from their experiences, and strive for excellence. To cultivate a feedback culture, consider implementing the following strategies:

- **Encourage regular feedback exchanges:** Make feedback an ongoing process rather than a one-time event. Schedule or attend regular opportunities for feedback, such as one-on-one meetings, team check-ins, or performance reviews. This ensures that you can receive timely and relevant feedback on your performance and development or provide constructive feedback to others.
- **Celebrate Growth and Progress Together**: Take the time to notice and appreciate the progress and accomplishments you and others have made. Remember that recognizing the effectiveness of feedback as a force for change can

boost motivation and remind everyone just how important it is to embrace feedback in our lives.
- **Promote open, honest, and respectful communication**: Lead by example by being open to receiving feedback and demonstrating a willingness to learn from your experiences. This sets a positive tone for others to embrace feedback. You can also emphasize the value of empathic listening, understanding, and collaboration when engaging in feedback exchanges.

Exercises

In this exercise, your task is to read each scenario carefully and determine which type of feedback, based on Carl Rogers' five types, would be the most appropriate to use in each situation. Remember that each scenario is unique, and the context plays a significant role in selecting the best feedback type. After you've made your choice, you can check your answer and read a brief explanation that provides the rationale behind the correct choice. This exercise will help you gain a deeper understanding of the various feedback types and their applications in different contexts.

Scenario: Imagine you are a team leader in a software development company. One of your team members, Jane, has been struggling with a complex coding task for the past week. She has been staying late in the office, trying to find a solution, but her frustration is evident. You have observed her dedication and hard work, but you also noticed that she could use some guidance to tackle the problem more efficiently. In this scenario, which type of feedback would be most appropriate to provide Jane?

Answer: Directive Feedback

Jane is facing a specific challenge that requires clear direction and assistance. By providing her with directive feedback, you can offer precise guidance, advice, or recommendations that will help her navigate the complexity of the task more effectively. This type of feedback is ideally suited for situations where individuals need explicit instructions to overcome obstacles or accomplish tasks. While offering directive feedback, it's important to maintain a balance and avoid undermining the recipient's sense of autonomy and self-efficacy.

Scenario: A colleague confides in you about their difficulties in navigating a complex workplace situation, unsure of how to handle it.

Answer: Probing Feedback (but other types may also be appropriate depending on the context)

Explanation: In this scenario, your colleague is seeking guidance and trying to make sense of a complicated situation. By offering probing feedback, you can provide alternative perspectives and help them gain a deeper understanding of the situation. This can lead to discovering possible solutions as it encourages self-reflection and understanding.

It's worth mentioning that there is no one-size-fits-all solution when it comes to feedback. Depending on the specifics of the situation and your colleague's needs, other types of feedback might also be appropriate. For example, if your colleague needs more explicit advice or guidance, directive feedback could be beneficial. Similarly, if your colleague requires encouragement and validation, supportive feedback might be the better choice.

The key takeaway is that while probing feedback can be a valuable tool in this scenario, it's crucial to consider the context and the individual's needs when determining the most suitable type of feedback to use. This means that you have to be flexible and adapt your approach as needed, being prepared to switch between different types of feedback on the fly to ensure the most effective and supportive response to your colleague's situation.

Chapter 2:
Giving Feedback

The manner in which you provide feedback is equally as significant as the message it conveys. The efficacy of feedback relies heavily not just on its content, but also on the intention behind it, the timing of its delivery, and the overall context. Their power, as integral parts of the feedback delivery process, will be the focal points of our discussion in this section. After establishing a strong understanding of these elements, we will transition into the exploration of the SBI (Situation-Behavior-Impact) model. This will serve as a practical guide to structure your feedback in a manner that is both effective and constructive.

Don't be afraid to give feedback. It can be a powerful tool for learning and growth when delivered effectively. Keep in mind that providing feedback effectively is a skill that requires practice and finesse. So, embrace the opportunity to help others grow, and trust in your ability to deliver feedback in a constructive and meaningful way.

The Power of Intention

At the core of effective feedback delivery is intention. The primary purpose of giving feedback should always be to help the other person grow and improve. This requires you to approach the feedback process with a positive, constructive mindset, focusing on the recipient's development rather than asserting power or control. When your intentions are clear and positive, the feedback you provide is more likely to be received with openness and gratitude, paving the way for meaningful change and growth.

For instance, imagine a manager providing feedback to a team member who has been struggling to meet deadlines. If the manager's intention is to help the team member improve their time management skills, they may offer specific suggestions for prioritizing tasks, delegating responsibilities, or using productivity tools. However, should the manager's intention be ambiguous or come across as negative - for instance, stating, "Can't you manage your time better?" - it may be perceived as overly controlling or judgmental. This makes the feedback look like a criticism rather than constructive guidance.

The Significance of Timing

Timing is another crucial factor in delivering feedback effectively. Choosing the right moment can mean the difference between a successful, growth-oriented conversation and a tense, unproductive exchange. It is essential to avoid sharing your feedback when emotions are running high, as this can cloud your judgment and prevent you from communicating your message clearly and empathetically. Similarly, you should avoid delivering feedback when the recipient is already feeling overwhelmed, as they may be unable to process the information and respond constructively.

To ensure that your feedback is well-received, you should look for moments when the recipient is calm, receptive, and open to learning. You can try scheduling a dedicated time to discuss feedback, allowing both parties to prepare mentally and emotionally for the conversation.

Understanding the Context

I already discussed how important context is in questioning, but it also plays a significant role in the feedback process. It is because it influences how your message is perceived and whether it leads to positive change. Before delivering feedback, you have to consider the environment and circumstances surrounding the situation. This includes factors such as the recipient's current workload, their emotional state, and any external pressures they may be facing. You should also be mindful of cultural and personal differences that may impact how your feedback is received, adapting your communication style accordingly to ensure your message is understood as intended.

The SBI Model

The Situation-Behavior-Impact (SBI) model offers a powerful, user-friendly tool for constructing and delivering effective feedback. It is a simple three-step approach that focuses on providing specific and objective feedback, making it easier for the recipient to understand and take action. Focusing on actual situations and visible behaviors makes feedback more meaningful and helpful. For instance, instead of saying, "You were unprofessional during the meeting," you could use the SBI model and say, "During yesterday's team meeting (situation), you interrupted others several times (behavior), which made it difficult for others to share their thoughts and ideas (impact)."

The model prevents your feedback from feeling like a personal attack as you are focusing on the individual's actions and not his personality. Here's an example. "Last week, when we were discussing the project deadline (situation), you raised your voice and seemed agitated (behavior), which made the team feel uncomfortable and less inclined to contribute their opinions (impact)."

Here are specific scenarios when this model is effective and should be used.

Performance Reviews

The SBI model is particularly useful during performance reviews, as it provides a structured framework for discussing an employee's strengths and areas for improvement. By focusing on specific situations and behaviors, both the reviewer and the employee can engage in a constructive dialogue about how to enhance performance and achieve goals.

Addressing Conflict

In situations where conflict arises, the SBI model can be used to address the issue in a non-confrontational manner. The model lets you talk about the problem, not the person. This avoids finger-pointing or blaming anyone personally by discussing the specific situation and the actions that happened instead. This approach keeps everyone focused on finding solutions and maintaining a positive team atmosphere. It's all about fixing the issue together, not finding someone to blame.

Coaching and Mentoring

A mentor or coach is not just an instructor but also someone who kindles transformation within the individual or team they are guiding. When they employ the SBI model, they give their mentees a clear, objective view of their actions. This helps those being mentored or coached to see the direct consequences of their actions, almost like experiencing an 'a-ha' moment.

So, when mentors and coaches embrace the SBI model, they're not just providing feedback - they're crafting memorable learning moments that can spark growth and development. This approach is less about 'teaching' and more about 'illuminating,' lighting up the path for individuals to journey towards their own growth.

Skill Development

When individuals are working on developing particular skills or competencies, the SBI model can also be utilized to provide specific feedback. By highlighting definitive situations, behaviors, and their impact, the individuals receiving the feedback can gain a clear understanding of their progress as well as areas that require further development.

Components

Knowing now the multiple scenarios where it can be used, let's take a deep dive into the core components of the SBI model and learn how to effectively integrate them into your feedback process so that it enhances your feedback's impact and value.

Situation

The first component of the SBI model is the **Situation**. A successful feedback conversation relies on a strong foundation, and that foundation is a clear context. The SBI model emphasizes the importance of pinpointing the specific situation in which the behavior occurred. Doing so allows both parties to have a shared understanding of the event, which is crucial for effective communication.

Establishing common ground prevents potential misunderstandings. When both parties recognize the situation being discussed, they are more likely to remain open and receptive to the conversation. This encourages an atmosphere of honesty, trust, and focus, making the feedback exchange more productive. For instance, consider the difference between these two statements. "You're always late," and "During last week's team meeting, you arrived 15 minutes after the scheduled start time." The first statement is vague and may lead the recipient to feel attacked or unfairly judged. In contrast, the second statement is specific and factual, making it easier for the recipient to recall the situation and recognize their behavior.

In order to incorporate this component in your feedback, you can do the following:

- ***Use concrete examples:*** Paint a clear picture of the specific event or circumstance you're addressing. This helps the recipient understand the context and makes it easier for them to recall the situation, leading to a more productive conversation.
- ***Avoid generalizations:*** Stay away from generalizations or vague descriptions, which can be easily misinterpreted or dismissed by the recipient. Instead, focus on the specifics of the situation to maintain a clear and accurate context for the feedback.
- ***Be timely:*** Give feedback as close to the event as possible, ideally within a day or two. This ensures that the situa-

tion is still fresh in both your mind and the recipient's mind, making it easier to discuss the details and work on improvement.

Behavior

The second component of the SBI model is the **Behavior**. It requires you to discuss specific, observable actions to eliminate the need for interpretation and reduce the chances of miscommunication. Making assumptions, instead of focusing on behavior, can easily lead to defensiveness, as the recipient may feel misunderstood or unfairly judged.

Imagine if someone said to you, "You didn't care about the project." That's a big assumption about what you feel, which could, in turn, make you defensive. But what if they said, "I noticed that you didn't submit your part of the project on time." That's just talking about what happened, not making guesses about your feelings. It makes it easier for you to think about what you did without feeling like someone's judging you personally.

To effectively apply this component of the SBI model, consider the following guidelines:

- *Be specific:* Describe the behavior in detail, using clear and straightforward language. This ensures that the recipient clearly understands what actions are being discussed.
- *Use neutral language:* Avoid emotionally charged words or phrases that may trigger a defensive response. Some examples of these would be, "I'm absolutely furious!" "I'm so disappointed in you." or "You're such a heartless person." Instead, use neutral language to create a non-threatening environment for the conversation.
- *Balance Specificity and Conciseness:* While being specific is crucial, overly detailed feedback can also be overwhelming. Strike a balance between the two. Provide enough

detail to be clear and actionable but keep it concise to maintain engagement.

Impact

The third and final component of the SBI model is the **Impact**. It especially emphasizes the impact of the behavior on other people. It involves explaining the consequences of the individual's actions on the team, project, or with other individuals. By doing so, you help the recipient understand the significance of their behavior. Doing so promotes a sense of responsibility and accountability.

Understanding the impact of one's actions can also promote empathy, as it allows the individual to see the situation from others' perspectives. As humans are relational beings and mostly do not want to cause harm or negative feelings to others, highlighting the consequence in feedback encourages positive change and facilitates personal and professional growth.

For instance, consider the following statement: "When you didn't submit your part of the project on time, it delayed the entire team's progress and led to additional stress for everyone involved." This feedback clearly outlines the consequences of the individual's behavior, enabling them to grasp the importance of timely submissions and the potential ripple effect on others.

To effectively convey the impact in a feedback conversation, here are tips you can use.

- *Highlight the ripple effect:* Explain how the behavior impacts not only the immediate situation but also the broader effects. This can help the individual realize the far-reaching implications of their actions.
- *Use "I" statements:* Express the impact from your perspective to convey your personal experience of the consequences. This approach can create a more empathetic and authentic connection with the recipient.

- ***Offer potential solutions:*** Discuss possible ways the individual could address the issue or improve their behavior, demonstrating your commitment to their growth and success.

The SBI model paves the way for genuine and constructive feedback discussions. The key is to establish the context of the situation, focus on the visible actions, and highlight their effects. This approach will build stronger, more productive dialogues.

Overcoming Feedback Challenges

Another thing to remember is that while feedback is vital, providing them can be fraught with challenges. Reactions to feedback can range from defensiveness and strong emotional responses to misinterpretation. In this section, we will explore how to overcome these common challenges when giving feedback, enabling you to foster productive and meaningful conversations that lead to positive change.

Defensiveness

Defensiveness often stems from a sense of vulnerability or fear of being judged. When someone perceives feedback as a threat to their self-esteem, their natural response is to protect themselves. This self-preservation instinct can manifest as denial, shifting blame, or avoiding responsibility. Once you recognize the underlying causes of defensiveness, you can better approach these situations and have a more open and constructive dialogue. Here are some strategies you can do to make a person more receptive to your feedback.

Build trust and create a safe environment for feedback: Creating a foundation of trust is important in addressing defensiveness since it can help the recipient feel more secure and receptive to feedback. Begin by expressing your intentions and emphasizing that the goal is to help the individual improve and grow. Show genuine care and support and highlight your shared commitment to success.

Provide balanced feedback: Feedback that only focuses on areas of improvement can be demoralizing. This, in turn, can trigger defensiveness. To counter this, ensure your feedback includes both positive reinforcement and areas for improvement. When people hear about their strengths or successes first, they may be more open to hearing about areas where they can improve. This approach creates a more balanced and less threatening dialogue.

Use the Situation, Behavior, Impact (SBI) model: As seen in the earlier sections, the model is an effective approach to delivering feedback in a non-threatening manner. This is because it helps recipients to look at the feedback not as a personal attack but rather as an attempt to promote an open and constructive conversation.

Emotional Reactions

It's crucial to recognize that feedback can evoke strong emotions, such as frustration, anger, or disappointment. Anticipating these emotional reactions allows you to approach the conversation with empathy and understanding. The first thing you should do after they express themselves is to validate the recipient's feelings. Do this by acknowledging their emotions and communicating your appreciation for their openness and honesty. You may say statements like:

- "It's understandable that you're feeling [emotion] given the circumstances."
- "I hear you and I understand why you're feeling [emotion]."
- "I can imagine how [emotion] this must be for you."
- "Your feelings are important, and it's okay to express them."
- "I want to validate your experience and the emotions you're going through."

Aside from the above statements, you can also do these techniques to manage emotional reactions to your feedback.

Maintain a calm and composed presence. Your demeanor when giving feedback can significantly influence the emotional climate. Regardless of the recipient's emotional response, it's imperative that you stay grounded and calm. Through this, you can help to diffuse tension and create a more balanced atmosphere for the discussion. Don't let your emotions get the best of you. Emotions spread. The person you're giving feedback to must see that you are calm and composed for them to also calm down.

Encourage the recipient to recognize and understand their emotions. This self-awareness can help them process their feelings and prevent emotional reactions from derailing the conversation. Offer support as they explore their feelings and emphasize the importance of growth and improvement. You can also highlight the potential benefits and opportunities to improve oneself through the help of feedback. This helps them reframe negative emotions as they are encouraged to look at the feedback as a learning experience.

Misinterpretation

The impact of feedback can be diminished if it is not communicated effectively, leading to misinterpretation and confusion. Misunderstanding feedback can also hinder progress and create tension in relationships.

Use concise language and examples. Provide clear and specific feedback with no room for interpretation. You should be straightforward and avoid complex terminologies such as technical jargon or ambiguous language. For instance, instead of saying, "The deliverables were not compliant with the predetermined benchmarks," simply say, "The work did not meet the set standards." They both communicate the same idea, but the latter use less formal language. The second feedback is easier to understand and will lead to less confusion and misunderstandings.

Be engaged. Pay close attention to the recipient's responses and provide opportunities for them to ask questions or seek clarification. Encourage open dialogue and be prepared to rephrase or elaborate on your feedback as needed. Doing these can help them understand you better.

Do follow-ups. At the end of the feedback conversation, confirm that the recipient understands the feedback and its implications. Ask them to summarize their takeaways and discuss any necessary action steps or changes. Additionally, schedule a follow-up conversation to revisit the feedback and assess progress. This ongoing dialogue can help ensure the feedback is fully comprehended and effectively implemented.

Cultural Barriers

Nowadays, it's common to find people from diverse cultural backgrounds working on projects together. This interconnectedness makes understanding and respecting other people's differences more important. Cultural barriers can significantly affect the process of giving and receiving feedback, sometimes leading to misinterpretation or unintended offense. Take these into consideration by doing these strategies.

Know the person. Before giving feedback to someone from a different cultural background, take the time to learn about their culture and communication norms. Understanding these nuances will help you tailor your feedback in a manner that aligns with their cultural values and expectations. Take note that some cultures may prioritize indirect communication and politeness, while others may appreciate directness and honesty.

For example, in many Asian cultures, people may be reserved and hesitant to express opinions openly. Directly confronting your Asian colleague might be seen as inappropriate and detrimental to your relationship. It's important to recognize that there are no rigid rules to follow when applying this strategy. There is no one-size-fits-all approach to providing feedback across different cultures. Be prepared to adapt your communication style and feedback techniques to suit the unique needs of each individual and situation.

Avoid using phrases rooted in specific cultures, in addition, you should steer clear of idiomatic expressions or culturally specific references that might be confusing to the recipient. Opt for clear, simple language that individuals from diverse cultural backgrounds can easily understand. Keep in mind that nonverbal cues, such as facial expressions, gestures, and body language, can communicate a significant amount of information. Still, their interpretation can vary greatly. Be mindful of the nonverbal signals you send, and make sure they align with the feedback you are providing.

Sensitive Feedback

Providing sensitive feedback involves addressing personal or delicate issues that require a high level of empathy, tact, and understanding. It involves taking into consideration the emotions and potential vulnerabilities of the recipient. When delivering sensitive feedback, make sure to:

Understand the person. it's essential to put yourself in the recipient's shoes and try to understand their feelings and emotions. Always approach these situations with care and consideration. Acknowledge their perspective and express your understanding of their situation. You should also show genuine concern and support throughout the conversation.

Choose a private and comfortable setting. Consider the environment and the circumstances surrounding the feedback. Make sure it's appropriate to the situation and that you're not blindsiding the recipient with unexpected feedback. Additionally, ensure the setting is conducive to an open and honest conversation, free from distractions or interruptions. Look for a place that has an atmosphere of privacy and confidentiality. This allows both you and the other party to speak openly and honestly without worrying about being overheard or judged by others.

To paint you a better picture, imagine that you need to address a colleague's persistent tardiness, which has been impacting the team's productivity. Instead of addressing the issue in the middle of the office or during a team meeting, where the person might feel embarrassed or defensive, arrange a one-on-one meeting in a quiet conference room or a neutral space like a coffee shop. By being mindful of the other person's feelings and delivering feedback in a considerate manner, you show respect for your colleague's feelings and emotions, creating a safe space for them to express their thoughts and concerns while preserving their self-esteem.

Exercises

To truly excel in giving feedback, it's crucial to practice and refine your skills. In this section, we'll explore some exercises designed to sharpen your abilities and make you a master of constructive feedback.

Crafting feedback using the SBI Model

Consider the following scenarios and create a feedback statement for each scenario using the SBI Model. This exercise will help you practice structuring feedback according to the Situation, Behavior, and Impact components.

1. A coworker frequently checks their phone during meetings, distracting the rest of the team.
2. A team member consistently exceeds their sales targets, positively impacting the team's overall performance.
3. A colleague often arrives late to work, causing delays in morning team meetings.
4. An employee has proactively taken on additional responsibilities, leading to a more efficient workflow for the team.

Example for Scenario 1:

- Situation: "During yesterday's team meeting,"
- Behavior: "I noticed that you were frequently checking your phone,"
- Impact: "this was distracting for the rest of the team and made it difficult to maintain focus on the discussion."

Putting it all together: "During yesterday's team meeting, I noticed that you were frequently checking your phone, which was distracting for the rest of the team and made it difficult to maintain focus on the discussion."

Overcoming Feedback Challenges

This exercise will help you practice overcoming various challenges in giving feedback. Consider how you can communicate the feedback respectfully, empathetically, and clearly.

Instructions:

1. Read each scenario and identify the challenge in giving feedback.
2. Write a feedback statement that addresses the challenge, considering the recipient's feelings, potential resistance, and any factors that may lead to misinterpretation or emotional reactions.
3. Reflect on how you tailored your feedback to overcome the challenge and consider how you might apply these strategies in future feedback situations.

Scenarios:

1. A coworker from a different cultural background seems hesitant to speak up during team meetings, despite consistently delivering high-quality work. You want to encourage them to share their ideas and contribute to discussions.
2. A colleague has been struggling with personal issues, which has led to a decline in their work performance. You

want to address the situation with compassion and understanding while emphasizing the importance of maintaining work standards.
3. A team member tends to dominate conversations during meetings, which can make it difficult for others to contribute. You want to address this behavior without causing the individual to feel singled out or attacked.
4. You need to provide feedback to an employee who has shown resistance to feedback in the past. The feedback is about their time management skills, which have led to missed deadlines and increased stress for the team.
5. A colleague has a strong emotional reaction whenever they receive feedback, even if it's constructive. You want to address their lack of attention to detail, which has led to errors in their work.

Chapter 3:
Receiving Feedback

Now that we're done tackling the art of giving feedback, it's time to flip the coin and discuss the art of receiving one. I understand that embracing feedback can be challenging. Humans often shy away from feeling judged or criticized as we take the opinions of others in high regard. However, don't look at feedback as a judgment of yourself but rather as a constructive comment that you can ponder on. Doing so can bring you rewards that are truly remarkable. In this section, we will start by discussing the importance of a growth mindset and how it intertwines with receiving feedback. Then we will look into the challenges in accepting feedback and I'll share my strategies to overcome them. Of course, I'll also teach you how to request feedback effectively and address them with a feedback action plan.

Growth Mindset in Relation to Feedback

A growth mindset, a concept pioneered by psychologist Carol Dweck (2006), emphasizes the belief that your abilities and intelligence can evolve through dedication, hard work, and learning from experiences. This mindset nurtures continuous learning and views challenges as stepping stones to growth. In contrast, a fixed mindset assumes that your abilities are innate and unchangeable, limiting your potential for personal and professional development.

How Feedback and Growth Mindset Relate to Each Other

Feedback and a growth mindset are deeply intertwined. By adopting a growth mindset, you become more open to feedback since it allows you to see criticism as an opportunity for growth rather than a personal attack. Conversely, by embracing feedback, you nurture your growth mindset since it gives you more information on areas where you need to improve on.

For example, in a professional setting, a manager with a growth mindset seeks feedback from their team members to identify areas for improvement in their leadership style. He can promote a more supportive and collaborative work environment by implementing the suggested changes, ultimately enhancing team performance. In a personal context, an individual that cultivates a growth mindset will ask for feedback from friends or family members to improve their communication skills. They can develop stronger relationships with others by listening to their suggestions and practicing new strategies.

Together, they create a positive feedback loop that builds resilience, adaptability, and ongoing development. By combining the power of constructive feedback with the principles of a growth mindset, you unlock your full potential.

Challenges in Receiving Feedback

It's hard when you are at the receiving end of feedback. It's common to feel lacking, disheartened, and frustrated when confronted with your shortcomings or areas for improvement. On top of that, there are also other emotional and psychological challenges that further hinder your ability to embrace and learn from the feedback you receive. In this section, we will explore these challenges, identifying the obstacles you can face when receiving feedback and providing strategies to overcome them.

Negative Emotional Reactions

One of the primary challenges in effectively receiving feedback is managing your emotional reactions. When you receive input that seems negative or critical, it can trigger a range of emotions, including defensiveness, resentment, and self-doubt. These emotional reactions can make it difficult for you to process and learn from the feedback.

This highlights the importance of ***practicing self-awareness and self-reflection***. When you notice an emotional reaction to feedback, take a step back and consider the source of your feelings. Assess the feedback objectively, evaluating its accuracy and relevance. If you find that your emotions are clouding your judgment, try to refocus on the content of the feedback and consider its potential value.

For instance, if you receive feedback suggesting that your project proposal lacks clarity, your initial reaction might be defensiveness or annoyance, as it could feel like your skills are lacking or you're not good at what you're doing. However, when you acknowledge your emotions and reflect on the feedback objectively, you begin to see that they are not attacking you personally. This shifts your perspective to view this feedback as a challenge and see it as an opportunity to enhance your communication skills and make your future project proposals more engaging and clear.

Relationship Dynamics

Another challenge in receiving feedback is navigating the complex dynamics of your relationships with the people providing the input. Your feelings towards the person giving the feedback can affect your receptiveness and willingness to learn from their advice.

To overcome this barrier, ***focus on the content of the feedback rather than the person delivering it,*** and ***don't take what they say personally.*** When you separate the feedback from the individual providing it, you can evaluate the information more objectively and avoid letting personal biases influence your interpretation.

Additionally, ***fostering strong, trusting relationships*** with your colleagues, mentors, and supervisors can help minimize the impact of relationship dynamics on feedback receptiveness. When trust is established, you are more likely to view the feedback as constructive and well-intended, even if it may be challenging to accept.

For instance, if a coworker with whom you have a tense relationship offers feedback on your team collaboration. Your immediate reaction may be to dismiss the feedback, attributing it to the personal issues between the two of you. This is a common response when feedback comes from someone whom you have a difficult relationship with.

However, when you focus on the content of the feedback and consider its potential value, you can learn from it and grow professionally, regardless of your personal feelings toward the person providing the feedback. Furthermore, this situation could serve as a starting point to mend your relationship with your colleague. You can approach them, thanking them for their feedback, and asking for further suggestions on how you could improve your work.

Feedback That Challenges Your Self-Perception

Receiving feedback that challenges your self-image or identity can be particularly difficult, as it can evoke feelings of insecurity or inadequacy. Such feedback may lead to self-doubt and shake your confidence in your skills and worth.

Cultivating self-compassion is essential when managing feedback that challenges your self-perception. Acknowledge your feelings but remind yourself that receiving feedback is a normal part of life and a necessary component of growth. Treat yourself with kindness and give yourself permission to be imperfect while committing to learning from the feedback and making necessary improvements. For example, suppose you receive feedback that suggests your leadership style is too controlling. In that case, it may trigger feelings of self-doubt and insecurity. By embracing a growth mindset and practicing self-compassion, you can acknowledge your feelings and use the feedback as an opportunity to refine your leadership skills and grow as a professional.

Asking for Feedback Effectively

Acknowledging that there is room for improvement is the first step toward personal and professional growth. The next step is to ask for feedback. It takes great courage to seek feedback yourself and shows your determination for self-development. In this chapter, I will teach you techniques for asking for feedback effectively. Mastering the skill of asking for feedback can help you gain the knowledge and understanding necessary to enhance your performance and achieve greater success.

Framing the Request

How you approach the conversation plays a significant role in determining the quality of the feedback you receive. When asking for feedback, frame the request in a manner that fosters open and honest communication.

Choosing the right moment to ask for feedback is important. Timing is crucial, as it ensures that the person providing feedback can give their undivided attention to your request. Are they busy? Are they stressed? Are they focusing on something else? Asking them during these times may lead to rushed or unhelpful responses.

Also, be specific about your goals and clearly state your objectives when seeking feedback. Emphasize on your commitment to personal and professional growth and explicitly express your appreciation for the other person's perspective. This approach helps create a positive atmosphere that promotes constructive feedback. Make use of open-ended questions to encourage thoughtful and detailed responses. Rather than asking, "Did I do a good job?" consider posing the question, "What could I have done differently to improve my performance?" This approach allows the person providing feedback to share their insights and observations more effectively, leading to more valuable and actionable input.

Focusing on Key Aspects of Growth

When seeking feedback, concentrate on specific areas where you believe you could improve. Focusing on particular aspects enables the person providing feedback to offer targeted, actionable suggestions. This makes the follow-through more effective for you. While it's natural to seek positive feedback, constructive criticism is often more valuable to make yourself better. Encourage those providing feedback to share their genuine thoughts on areas where you could enhance your performance, even when this could hurt or offend you. In turn, you should be open to their suggestions. To identify areas of improvement, start by reflecting on your strengths and weaknesses. Assess your performance honestly and determine which aspects of your work you excel in and where you could use some improvement. This self-awareness allows you to ask for feedback that directly addresses your needs.

Seeking Detailed Feedback

Receiving specific and detailed suggestions can maximize the benefits of the feedback process. This can help you better understand how to address their feedback and identify the parts where you need to make adjustments.

Another tip is to concentrate on your behavior rather than your personality traits when seeking feedback. For example, instead of asking if you're a good team player, inquire about actions that could make you more effective in a team setting. Focus on specific projects or tasks you have recently completed instead of asking for general feedback. This approach enables the person providing feedback to reflect on concrete examples, making their input more relevant and actionable.

Turning Feedback into Action

Once you've received feedback, the next step is to turn that information into actionable steps that will help you grow and develop. This involves creating a feedback action plan, tracking your progress, and celebrating your successes. In this section, we will explore each of these components in detail to help you make the most of the feedback you receive.

Creating a Feedback Action Plan

A feedback action plan is a structured approach to addressing the suggestions and insights you receive from others. It provides a roadmap for you to track your growth and helps you prioritize your goals. Here's how to create an effective feedback action plan:

1. Identify Key Areas for Improvement

Start by carefully reviewing the feedback you received, focusing on the most critical areas for growth. Consider which aspects of your personal or professional life will benefit the most from addressing these areas. For example, suppose you receive feedback that your presentation skills need improvement. In that case, you can prioritize improving your ability to communicate effectively and make a stronger impact in your career.

2. Set SMART Goals for Improvement

With the key areas identified, it's time to develop specific, measurable, achievable, relevant, and time-bound (SMART) goals for each area of improvement. By setting SMART goals, you create clear, attainable objectives that will keep you focused and motivated.

You can use this as a guide.

- **S - Specific:** Clearly define the goal, outlining what you want to accomplish.
- **M - Measurable**: Determine how you will track progress and quantify the goal's achievement.
- **A - Achievable:** Ensure the goal is realistic, considering available resources and constraints.
- **R - Relevant:** Align the goal with your broader objectives, values, and priorities.
- **T - Time-bound:** Set a deadline to create a sense of urgency and maintain motivation.

Now that you have your SMART goals in place, break them down into smaller, manageable tasks that you can work on consistently. This will help you make steady progress and see tangible results, boosting your motivation and self-confidence. For example, you could set a SMART goal like "deliver a confident and engaging presentation to my team within the next two months." Breaking down your goal of improving your presentation skills, the actionable steps may include:

- Attending a public speaking workshop.
- Practicing your speech in front of a mirror.
- Seeking feedback from a trusted colleague.

3. Establish a Timeline for Success

Create a timeline for completing each step in your action plan. This helps you stay on track, maintain momentum, and avoid procrastination. Regularly review your timeline and adjust it as needed to accommodate any changes or challenges that may arise. Using the presentation skills example, you could set a deadline for attending the workshop within the next month and practicing your speech at least once a week.

4. Build a Support Network

One of the most fundamental human needs is the need to belong and to be understood. A support group addresses this need. In such a network, you're heard and recognized for who you are, not just for the problem you're facing.

Share your feedback action plan with trusted friends, mentors, or colleagues who can offer guidance, encouragement, and accountability. They can provide practical advice, share strategies that have worked for them, and keep you motivated when progress seems slow or obstacles seem high.

For example, within your support network, there could be a colleague who has a knack for public speaking and delivering impressive presentations. This colleague has likely developed their skills over time, learning from both successes and failures. Sharing your action plan with them could prompt them to offer guidance based on their personal experiences. They might even share tips for keeping an audience engaged, tricks for calming presentation nerves, or techniques for creating visually impactful slides.

Here is a template for you to use. Tweak it according to what you need and prefer:

Feedback Received	Provide a summary of the feedback you received, including the key points and suggestions for improvement.
Goals	Clearly state your overall goals or objectives that you want to achieve through implementing the feedback. Make sure to follow the S.M.A.R.T. goals guidelines.

Actions To Take	List the specific actions you'll be doing to address the feedback and achieve your goals. For each action item, include the following information.	
	Action #1	Write a specific action you'll be doing to address the feedback and reach your goals
	Priority	Assign a priority level (e.g., high, medium, low) to each action item based on its importance or urgency.
	Deadline	Set a target date for completing the action item.
Progress Tracking	Describe how you will track your progress on each action item, such as regular progress reports, journal entries, or feedback from colleagues.	

Example:

Feedback Received	My presentation skills need improvement. I must work on my effective communication and make impactful presentations.	
Goals	Deliver a confident and engaging presentation to my team within the next three months	
Actions To Take	Action #1	Attend a public speaking workshop
	Priority	Medium
	Deadline	Within the next 2 months
Progress Tracking	Ask a colleague to rate my skills before the next presentation	

Keeping Track of Your Progress

After creating your plan, you now have to monitor your progress to ensure that your feedback action plan remains relevant and effective. This is because as you progress, new challenges may arise, requiring you to revise your approach or set new goals. Regular tracking of your progress enables you to identify areas where you may need to adjust your approach or seek additional support. One way to do this is by maintaining a progress journal in which you document your achievements and challenges.

Another strategy is to continuously seek feedback from colleagues, mentors, and supervisors to gauge your progress and look at it from a different perspective. Ongoing feedback provides valuable insights and helps you stay on track toward achieving your goals.

Celebrating Success

As you work towards your growth, it's also important to recognize how far you have come and to celebrate your successes, both big and small. Reflect on the progress you've made and the goals you've accomplished. This self-reflection can boost your confidence and sense of pride. At the same time, it also reinforces the value of incorporating feedback into your growth journey.

Share your achievements with colleagues, mentors, and supervisors. This helps you build connections and demonstrates your commitment to continuous improvement as you show them that you take their words seriously. Rewarding yourself for reaching milestones or achieving specific goals is a great way to maintain motivation and excitement throughout your journey. These rewards can be simple acts of self-care or treats that help you stay engaged and motivated.

Exercise

Now let's put everything you learned into action! Here is an exercise that can help you act upon the feedback given to you.

Active Listening [3 in 1]

Instructions:

1. Reflect on a recent feedback you received, whether it's from a colleague, supervisor, or friend. Write down the feedback in the SBI format (Situation, Behavior, Impact).
2. Identify the key area(s) for improvement based on the feedback. Write down 2-3 specific aspects you want to focus on.
3. For each aspect, brainstorm at least two actionable steps you can take to address it. Consider seeking resources, setting goals, or working on relevant skills.
4. Prioritize the actionable steps based on urgency and importance. Assign deadlines for completing each step and create a timeline.
5. Share your action plan with a trusted colleague, mentor, or friend, and ask for their feedback and suggestions. Make any necessary adjustments to your plan based on their input.
6. Begin implementing your action plan and regularly review your progress. Adjust your plan as needed and continue seeking feedback to refine your approach.
7. By the end of this exercise, you should have a clear action plan that outlines how you'll address feedback that you receive. I hope that you can then apply this in real situations.

Conclusion

As you reach the conclusion of this book, you've taken the first step in your journey toward mastering the art of active listening. It's my sincere hope that the knowledge and techniques shared within these pages will be of immense value to you. Remember, active listening is a deeply personal and subjective practice. While not every piece of advice may resonate with everyone, this book intends to provide you with a solid foundation and the necessary tools to navigate your unique path.

This book aims not only to provide you with specific techniques and strategies but also to foster the development of the skills needed to handle the complexities of communication and relationships on your own terms. Though it may be tempting to view this book as a definitive guide, the true power of active listening lies in your ability to adapt and grow with the experiences and challenges you face along the way.

Of course, this doesn't mean that you should cast this book aside. The insights and guidance offered within these pages are genuine and designed to support your journey toward becoming a more effective listener. As you progress and face new obstacles, you may find yourself returning to this book as a valuable resource. With that in mind, I would like to leave you with a summary of the key takeaways from each sub-book, serving as a useful reference point for future reflection. Of course, you are always welcome to revisit the entirety of the book as often as you like.

The first sub-book delved into the essential skill of empathic listening. I began by providing an overview of empathic listening and its importance in fostering understanding and deeper connections with others. I also highlighted the differences between this listening style to other types, emphasizing the need for genuine emotional engagement and empathy when practicing it.

Aside from this, a significant portion of this sub-book was dedicated to helping you develop self-awareness, emotional intelligence, and empathy. I also discussed various exercises and strategies that can help you become more attuned to your own emotions and those of others. By honing these skills, you'll be better equipped to practice empathic listening and respond to the emotional needs of those around you.

Lastly, we delved into its application in various aspects of life, such as strengthening bonds with family and friends, navigating conflicts, and enhancing teamwork in the workplace. Moreover, I emphasized the importance of continuous improvement, self-reflection, and seeking feedback to refine your empathic listening skills, ensuring you grow as a compassionate and effective communicator.

The second sub-book, focused on thought-provoking questions, a vital component of communication after empathic listening. It helps you develop your questioning skills, which since asking thoughtful and meaningful questions can lead to deeper connections and more effective conversations.

We then explored various questioning techniques and strategies that can be employed in different contexts. Open-ended questions were identified as valuable tools for encouraging dialogue and generating more information, while closed-ended questions were acknowledged as useful for obtaining specific details or confirming understanding. We also examined probing questions, which encourage the elaboration and exploration of ideas, and Socratic questioning, a technique that is rooted in critical thinking and self-reflection.

Additionally, I provided practical tips for navigating and elevating conversations with thought-provoking questions. We explored the

Five Golden Tips of Questioning, which have been found to be incredibly helpful in facilitating engaging and insightful conversations. We looked at each tip in detail, complete with examples from real-life experiences, to give you a clear idea of how to implement these strategies in your own conversations.

In the final sub-book, I addressed the art of giving and receiving constructive feedback for personal and professional growth. I started by discussing the various types, purposes, and contexts of feedback, highlighting the importance of understanding the differences between feedback styles and adapting your approach accordingly.

A crucial aspect of feedback mastery is establishing a feedback culture built on trust and openness. I provided strategies for fostering a positive environment where feedback is welcomed and valued, emphasizing the need for clear communication and mutual respect. i also introduced the SBI (Situation, Behavior, Impact) model, a practical tool for structuring feedback in a way that is specific, objective, and focused on the impact of the behavior in question.

To further support your feedback mastery journey, I addressed common challenges faced when giving feedback, such as dealing with defensiveness or resistance, and provided strategies for overcoming these obstacles. I also emphasized the importance of clearness, empathy, and support while delivering constructive feedback.

On the receiving end, we explored the value of embracing feedback for growth. I discussed the importance of being open to feedback, strategies to overcome challenges of receiving feedback and techniques for asking for feedback effectively. By adopting a receptive attitude towards feedback, you'll be better positioned to learn from it and make meaningful improvements in your life.

Lastly, we examined how to turn feedback into action. I guided you on creating a feedback action plan and tracking your progress, ensuring that the insights gained from the process lead to tangible growth and development.

To make the most out of this book, I'd like to offer two tips on how to take full advantage of the information and techniques presented throughout the pages after reading. I hope that these suggestions will help you get the most out of your reading experience and facilitate the integration of active listening concepts into your daily life.

The first is by creating a personalized study plan tailored to your learning preferences and schedule. Set aside dedicated time to read and practice the techniques, and commit to reviewing the material regularly. By having a structured approach, you'll be more likely to absorb and retain the information, ultimately helping you to become a better active listener.

And the second and, I believe, the most effective way to improve your active listening skills is through practice. Make a conscious effort to apply the techniques you've learned in your daily conversations, whether at home, work, or in social settings. Remember that it's normal to encounter challenges or feel awkward at first – this is all part of the learning process. With time and consistent practice, your active listening skills will become more refined and natural.

As you continue your journey toward active listening mastery, let this book serve as a guiding resource and a source of inspiration. Remember that the path to mastery requires time, dedication, and consistent practice. Still, the rewards – in the form of deeper connections, improved communication, and personal growth – are well worth the effort.

Active listening is an ever-evolving skill; there will always be more to learn and discover. Stay curious and keep exploring new techniques, approaches, and ideas to further enhance your active listening abilities. Challenge yourself to push beyond your comfort zone and engage in conversations that will test your skills and stimulate your personal growth.

Don't hesitate to share your experiences and learnings with others when you gain proficiency in these skills. We can collectively create a more empathetic and understanding world by fostering a supportive community of active listeners.

Every now and then, celebrate your progress along the way. Recognize the milestones you have achieved, and take pride in the improvements you have made in your active listening abilities. By acknowledging your accomplishments, you will stay motivated and inspired to continue on your path toward mastery.

Finally, I want to thank you for embarking on this journey with me. I hope the insights and techniques shared in this book will serve as valuable tools as you continue developing your active listening skills. I encourage you to revisit the book as often as needed, and I wish you the very best in your ongoing quest for mastery.

Techniques & Tips Recap

The following are the techniques and tips found in *"Active Listening [3-in-1]"*:

#	Name	Explanation
1	**Finding Common Ground**	Listening to each other's perspectives and empathizing to find a mutually beneficial solution in disagreements.
2	**Empathy Through Acknowledgment**	Empathize by acknowledging another person's feelings.
3	**Perspective-Taking**	Imagine the experiences, emotions, and reasoning of someone with a different belief or opinion.
4	**Self-Understanding**	Identify and comprehend your emotions, strengths, weaknesses, and triggers.
5	**Emotion Management**	Effectively handle emotions and responses to remain composed in varying circumstances.
6	**Goal Persistence**	Stay motivated and committed to goals despite challenges or setbacks.
7	**Relationship Building Skills**	Develop communication, conflict resolution, and collaboration skills for strong relationships.
8	**Engaging Affirmatively**	Offer affirmative responses and feedback to demonstrate engagement.
9	**Self-Awareness in Listening**	Practice self-awareness and regulation to listen empathically without emotional interference.
10	**Active Listening Reminder**	Remind yourself to connect personally with the speaker, not just listen passively.

Active Listening [3 in 1]

#	Name	Explanation
11	Respecting Confidentiality	Respect privacy by not sharing learned information about someone without permission.
12	Attentive Scheduling	If preoccupied, suggest a later time for conversation to ensure attention.
13	Ensuring Understanding	Make sure the speaker feels heard and understood before offering guidance.
14	Reflective Summarization	Reflect and summarize the speaker's message to confirm understanding and demonstrate engagement.
15	Embracing Silence	Use silence to let the speaker navigate their emotions and articulate their experience.
16	Silent Engagement Signals	Maintain eye contact and use nonverbal cues like nodding to show engagement during silence.
17	Expressing Gratitude	Thank the person for sharing their thoughts and emotions after a conversation.
18	Clarifying with Questions	Use well-crafted questions to clarify ideas, uncover assumptions, and gain deeper insights.
19	Comfort with Ambiguity	Be comfortable with uncertainty to explore new questions, ideas, and possibilities.
20	Curious Observation	Practice observing the world with an open and curious mind.
21	Worldly Exposure	Expand your understanding by exposing yourself to diverse ideas, cultures, and experiences.
22	Mindfulness Enhancement	Incorporate practices like meditation or journaling to sharpen curiosity and inquisitiveness.
23	Commitment to Learning	Pursue ongoing learning through personal/professional goals, workshops, online courses, or hobbies.

#	Name	Explanation
24	**Question Evaluation**	Regularly assess the quality and intent of questions asked in conversations and interactions.
25	**Exploring New Interests**	Actively seek new topics, disciplines, or hobbies that spark your interest.
26	**Creativity Promotion**	Engage in creative activities like painting, writing, or music to boost creativity.
27	**Cultural Immersion**	Travel to new places to experience different cultures, environments, and perspectives.
28	**Surround with Curiosity**	Spend time with inquisitive individuals to fuel your own enthusiasm for learning and exploration.
29	**Insight Recording**	Keep a notebook or digital document to record questions, observations, and insights.
30	**Critical Response Analysis**	Scrutinize answers for logic and relevance, and ask follow-up questions for clarity.
31	**Attentive Follow-Up**	Listen closely and build upon answers with additional questions or connections.
32	**Prompting Deeper Thought**	Encourage deeper consideration of responses to explore different aspects of a topic.
33	**Viewpoint Appreciation**	Show understanding and respect for others' viewpoints, even when differing.
34	**Clarification Seeking**	Ask for further explanation or clarification when unsure about a response.
35	**Purpose-Driven Inquiry**	Identify the purpose of your question before asking.
36	**Simplicity in Questioning**	Aim for simplicity and clarity in your questions.

Active Listening [3 in 1]

#	Name	Explanation
37	Light-Hearted Informal Queries	Use easygoing questions in informal settings to foster relaxed discussions.
38	Professional Question Focus	In professional settings, ask specific, goal-oriented questions related to the task.
39	Empathetic Sensitive Questioning	Choose empathetic and supportive questions for sensitive topics to respect others' feelings.
40	Stimulating Educational Questions	Ask thought-provoking questions in educational contexts to encourage critical thinking and deeper understanding.
41	Unconventional Questioning	Be open to asking unique or unusual questions to enrich the conversation.
42	Timely Questioning	Look for natural breaks or transitions in conversation to introduce questions.
43	Tone Matching	Ensure your tone aligns with the context of the conversation.
44	Respectful Inquiry with Strangers	When speaking to strangers, be genuinely curious but also considerate of their comfort and privacy.
45	Avoid Redundant Questions	Refrain from asking questions when you already know the answers.
46	Interpretive Feedback	Don't hesitate to give feedback to clarify your understanding.
47	Continuous Feedback	Make feedback a regular and ongoing activity.
48	Recognizing Progress	Take time to acknowledge and appreciate progress and achievements.
49	Feedback Receptiveness	Lead by example in receiving feedback and showing a willingness to learn.
50	Receptive Feedback Timing	Offer feedback when the recipient is calm and open to learning.

#	Name	Explanation
51	**Focused Feedback**	Base feedback on specific situations and observable behaviors for more impact.
52	**Prompt Feedback**	Give feedback as soon after the event as possible.
53	**Avoid Emotional Triggers**	Steer clear of words or phrases that could incite a defensive reaction.
54	**Detailed Yet Concise Feedback**	Provide clear, actionable feedback while keeping it concise.
55	**Personal Impact Expression**	Share how the situation or behavior affected you personally.
56	**Constructive Improvement Suggestions**	Suggest ways for the individual to address issues or enhance their behavior, showing support for their development.
57	**Maintaining Composure**	Stay calm and grounded, regardless of the recipient's emotional response.
58	**Feedback Understanding Confirmation**	Confirm that the feedback and its implications are understood at the end of the conversation.
59	**Cultural Sensitivity in Feedback**	Learn about cultural and communication norms before giving feedback to someone from a different background.
60	**Emotion Management in Feedback**	If emotions affect your judgment, refocus on the content and potential value of the feedback.
61	**Objective Feedback Reception**	Focus on the feedback content, not the person giving it, and avoid taking it personally.
62	**Self-Compassion and Imperfection**	Treat yourself kindly, allow imperfections, and commit to learning and improving from feedback.
63	**Focused Feedback Seeking**	Seek feedback on specific areas for potential improvement.

Active Listening [3 in 1]

#	Name	Explanation
64	**Progress Tracking**	Regularly monitor your progress to adjust strategies or seek extra support as needed.
65	**Milestone Rewards**	Reward yourself for achieving milestones or goals to stay motivated and enthusiastic on your journey.

Exclusive Bonuses

Dear Reader,

I am thrilled to introduce you to five enriching bonuses accompanying "Effective Feedback Strategies: Mastering the Art of Active Listening." These resources are tailored to deepen your understanding and enhance your skills in active listening and communication.

- **Bonus 1 - Key Terms Compendium: A Glossary for Active Listening.** This glossary demystifies the terminology of active listening, making it easier to grasp and apply these concepts in real-life scenarios.

- **Bonus 2 - Effective Feedback Strategies: Mastering the Art of Active Listening.** This short book offers insightful techniques and templates to provide constructive feedback, crucial for meaningful conversations.

- **Bonus 3 - Listen & Learn: Quizzes for Mastering Active Listening.** Engage with quizzes designed to test and reinforce your mastery of active listening skills, offering a fun and interactive learning experience.

- **Bonus 4 - The Listener's Path: A Reflective Journal for Mindful Communication** is a reflective journal for mindful communication, encouraging you to introspect and record your active listening journey, fostering self-awareness and growth.

- **Bonus 5 - Harmony Within: Guided Meditation and Mindfulness Exercises for Mastering Active Listening.** Delve into guided meditations and mindfulness exercises.

These are crafted to enhance your focus and presence, key components of effective active listening.

These bonuses are your toolkit for becoming an exceptional communicator. Embrace these resources to transform your interactions and build stronger, more empathetic connections.

How to Access Your Bonuses:

Scan the QR Code Below: Simply use your phone's camera or a QR code reader to scan the code, and you'll be directed straight to the bonus content.

Visit the Link: You can also access these valuable resources by visiting https://bit.ly/Weber-AL

Embark on a Path to Enhanced Communication!

These bonuses are designed to enrich your journey in mastering active listening, a vital life skill for all ages. I'm confident they will bolster your understanding and application of these techniques, empowering you in both personal and professional realms. Thank you for joining me on this journey towards effective communication, fostering deeper understanding, and building stronger connections through the art of active listening.

Warm regards,

Emma Leigh Weber

Resources

Allen, M. (2017). The SAGE Encyclopedia of Communication Research Methods. *SAGE Publications, Inc. eBooks.* https://doi.org/10.4135/9781483381411

Bhave, D. P., Teo, L. H., & Dalal, R. S. (2020). Privacy at Work: A Review and a Research Agenda for a Contested Terrain. *Journal of Management, 46*(1), 127–164. https://doi.org/10.1177/0149206319878254

Bonaccio, S., O'Reilly, J., O'Sullivan, S., & Chiocchio, F. (2016). Nonverbal Behavior and Communication in the Workplace. *Journal of Management, 42*(5), 1044–1074. https://doi.org/10.1177/0149206315621146

Bruce, J. (2022, January 18). The Empathy Deficit And Your Bottom Line. *Forbes.* https://www.forbes.com/sites/janbruce/2022/01/18/the-empathy-deficit-and-your-bottom-line/?sh=740e5d291674

Burns, L. (n.d.). *The Art and Heart of the Socratic Method: Connecting through Questioning, Listening, and Silence* [Conference Session]. https://core.ac.uk/download/pdf/32452111.pdf

Camino, L, Zeldin, S, Payne-Jackson, A. (1995). Basics of qualitative interviews and focus groups . Washington, D.C: Center for Youth Development and Policy Research, Academy for Educational Development.

Chin, C., & Osborne, J. (2008). Students' questions: a potential resource for teaching and learning science. *Studies in Science Education, 44*(1), 1–39. https://doi.org/10.1080/03057260701828101

De Waal, F. *The Evolution of Empathy*. (2005). Greater Good. https://greatergood.berkeley.edu/article/item/the_evolution_of_empathy

Dixit, A. (2018). Communication is Incomplete without Feedback. *Pen Acclaims, Volume 2*. http://www.penacclaims.com/wp-content/uploads/2018/08/Archit-Dixit.pdf

Goldsmith, D. J. (2000). Soliciting advice: The role of sequential placement in mitigating face threat. *Communication Monographs, 67*(1), 1–19. https://doi.org/10.1080/03637750009376492

Graesser, A. C., & Person, N. K. (1994). Question Asking During Tutoring. *American Educational Research Journal, 31*(1), 104–137. https://doi.org/10.3102/00028312031001104

Horowitz, L. N., Krasnoperova, E. N., Tatar, D., Hansen, M. F., Person, E. C., Galvin, K., & Nelson, K. N. (2001). The Way to Console May Depend on the Goal: Experimental Studies of Social Support. *Journal of Experimental Social Psychology, 37*(1), 49–61. https://doi.org/10.1006/jesp.2000.1435

Huang, K. E., Yeomans, M., Brooks, A. S., Minson, J. A., & Gino, F. (2017). It doesn't hurt to ask: Question-asking increases liking. *Journal of Personality and Social Psychology, 113*(3), 430–452. https://doi.org/10.1037/pspi0000097

Jug, R., Jiang, X. S., & Bean, S. M. (2019). Giving and Receiving Effective Feedback: A Review Article and How-To Guide. *Archives of Pathology & Laboratory Medicine, 143*(2), 244–250. https://doi.org/10.5858/arpa.2018-0058-ra

Lane, W. (2021, December 12). How do open-ended questions improve interpersonal communication? *Medium*. https://drwilliamlane.medium.com/how-do-open-ended-questions-improve-interpersonal-communication-7bdef30d0604

Li, N., & Yan, J. (2009). The effects of trust climate on individual performance. *Frontiers of Business Research in China, 3*(1), 27–49. https://doi.org/10.1007/s11782-009-0002-6

Misra, S., Cheng, L., Genevie, J., & Yuan, M. (2016a). The iPhone Effect. *Environment and Behavior, 48*(2), 275–298. https://doi.org/10.1177/0013916514539755

Moore, E. (2020). *Being Listened to With Empathy: The Experience and Effect for Emerging and Middle-Aged Adults* [Thesis].

Pfeiffer, J. W. (1998). *The Pfeiffer Library: Vol. Volume 6* (2nd Edition) [Book]. Pfeiffer & Company Library.

RSA. (2013, July 4). *RSA Replay - The Power of Vulnerability* [Video]. YouTube. https://www.youtube.com/watch?v=QMzB-v35HbLk

Rogers, C. R. (1961). On becoming a person: A therapist's view of psychotherapy. Boston, MA: Houghton Mifflin.

Rogers, C. R. (1970). On encouter groups. New York, NY: Harper & Row.

Singer, T., & Lamm, C. (2009). The Social Neuroscience of Empathy. *Annals of the New York Academy of Sciences, 1156*(1), 81–96. https://doi.org/10.1111/j.1749-6632.2009.04418.x

Use Situation-Behavior-Impact (SBI)™ to Understand Intent. CCL. https://www.ccl.org/articles/leading-effectively-articles/closing-the-gap-between-intent-vs-impact-sbii/

Weaver, J. C., Watson, K. W., & Barker, L. L. (1996). Individual differences in listening styles: Do you hear what I hear? *Personality and Individual Differences, 20*(3), 381–387. https://doi.org/10.1016/0191-8869(95)00194-8

Yeomans, M., Brooks, A. S., Huang, K. E., Minson, J. A., & Gino, F. (2019). It helps to ask: The cumulative benefits of asking follow-up questions. *Journal of Personality and Social Psychology, 117*(6), 1139–1144. https://doi.org/10.1037/pspi0000220

Made in the USA
Las Vegas, NV
31 August 2024

94618259R00085